BL🌼🌼M
TODAY
WORKBOOK

by:
Paula Mosher Wallace
Ginny Priz, CPLC

Published by Bloom Publishing, an imprint of Bloom In The Dark, Inc.

Bloom Today Workbook

Cover Design & Interior Formatting: Ginny Priz
Editing: Elizabeth Garrett
Paperback edition, Published September 1, 2019

ISBN-13: 978-0-9965309-6-5
ISBN-10: 0-9965309-6-7

www.bloominthedark.org

Scripture references are limited quotes from the online versions of these Bibles:

New International Version
King James Version
New King James Version
New Living Translation
Berean Study Bible
New American Standard Bible
English Standard Version
Christian Standard Bible

Table of Contents

Acknowledgments

This television show and workbook would not be possible without Monica Schmelter and the WHTN/CTN television station. Monica's faith and obedience opened the door for Bloom Today to be produced with excellence and broadcast throughout the Nashville, TN area.

Special thanks to Lisa Mouradian at Inspiration TV for following God, believing in us, and recognizing the need for this "taboo" content to offer hope to God's children around the world.

Thank you to Elizabeth Garrett for contributing her amazing editing skills.

Foreword

This article, published in the July 2017 issue of The Nashville Christian Family Magazine, tells the story of how God launched this television show.

The power went out as I stepped off the porch and into the garden. Something stabbed my leg. Ouch! That really hurt. I leaned down to feel for blood and hit my head on something concrete. As I fell, I grabbed at anything to break my fall. My hand caught on some material. I was glad until I heard someone scream, "let go of me!!" Before I realized what was happening, I was sprawled halfway between drowning in the lake and lost in stabbing thorns and weeds.

Disoriented in a place I'd never seen, I started crying. I hurt everywhere. I had no idea how to get help. Who knew what other dangers surrounded me. And I was too embarrassed to ask for help. Suddenly, the lights turned back on. I started laughing hysterically. I looked like a mess, but there was no blood. The lake was just a puddle. The thorns were just rose bushes. I would have some swelling and bruises, but I was fine. The porch was only five feet away. In a few weeks, I would be laughing as I told this story.

Light has the ability to help us see things for what they are, not what we feel like they could be. The new CTN/WHTN TV show, Bloom Today, is about shining light into the darkness of brokenness and abuse. "Once you know what the damage is, how it's caused, how to get help, and how to heal, you have so much more hope," says Ginny Priz, the anchor for the show. "Bloom Today is based on Ephesians 5:8-13 which tells us to shine light into the darkness so people will see darkness for what it is and know that the light brings good fruit." Priz continued.

Ginny Priz and her co-host, Paula Mosher Wallace, have a lot of personal experience in the areas of external and internal brokenness. They believe everyone should be a part of shining light into the darkness for the safety and healing of the hurting men and women that hide in plain sight.

"The more we understand about brokenness and abuse in our neighborhoods and churches, the more we can help everyone recognize it, heal from it, and start preventing it," said Priz. "When I realized that my pain was valid and I wasn't the only one hurting, I started being more honest about my pain. Then, others were able to begin helping me with the long journey to healing."

Priz admitted that being born with only part of her right arm was an obvious sign of external brokenness. Because her parents had always told her that God had specifically designed her that way, she was comfortable with her unique appearance. The internal brokenness took much longer to identify and begin to process for healing.

As Priz worked through much of her healing through Celebrate Recovery (CR), a Christian 12 step program, she learned that codependence and fear were the roots of her struggles with addictions and dysfunctional relationships. Using her recovery to help others, through being a sponsor and leader in CR, Priz realized the power of telling her story to help others find hope and healing.

Priz, in addition to being the Anchor for Bloom Today, is a Certified Professional Life Coach, instructor for several online courses, a public speaker, and the author of Ditch the Drama: How to Access God's Promises of Joy and Freedom no Matter What the World Throws at You. Even though she isn't being paid for most of the work she does, Priz has built her life around her calling from God to minister to the broken.

"I'm living by faith," Priz said. "God has told me to use my skills to help those who feel alone and hopeless instead of building a platform to make money. This can feel scary in a culture that is built around finding security in money and success, but I know that God will provide everything I need to do what He's asked me to do."

When asked why others ignore the issues of addictions, abuse, and dysfunction that affect more that half the population around us, Priz said, "It's uncomfortable to face our own brokenness, much less feel the pain of those around us. We'd rather live in a bubble of denial, distract ourselves with success, and complain about our stress levels. Anything is better than facing the reality of our pain."

Wallace agrees. "When I admitted to having been raped at the age of five by a man in my church, the female pastor I was talking to, told me 'Don't ever say that again. By admitting it, you are glorifying Satan.'" Wallace continued to explain how she had been abused in different ways from the age of two--by men and women who were in and out of her church. "I was abused sexually, physically, emotionally, verbally, and spiritually by a variety of people over a forty year span. Yes, all those types of abuse. By both men and women."

Afraid of what others would think, Wallace hid inside a shell of performance. A successful business owner and manager in a variety of industries, Wallace began to develop increasingly more severe health issues, anxiety and depression. As God began to heal her spirit, soul, and body, she realized that shame, guilt and fear had contributed to her illnesses.

Despite having been raised as a Christian, Wallace had grown up believing she deserved the abuse. "Even though I was born in Peru on the mission field, and grew up in a Christian community, I never understood that God didn't want me being the victim of abuse. I thought everyone else was just better at coping with the pain in their lives. It started so young, that I thought it was normal."

"My parents never deliberately hurt us, but growing up in a cult made me more vulnerable to abusive people around me." Wallace said. "Of course, as a perpetual victim, I learned that abuse can be found anywhere. No ethnic group, socioeconomic group, educational level or religious belief prevents abusers from hurting victims they have control over."

After Wallace moved to Franklin, God started prompting her to help others in ways she wished she had been helped. An avid reader, Wallace wanted to write a book that would tell true stories like hers. Despite not having written creatively in decades, Wallace began to interview women who had been healed from horrific damage.

"After prompting her to share her story, God connected me to each woman in a unique way. I got to write or edit stories from girls and women who represented different ages, ethnicities, cultures and educational levels," Wallace stated. "Evidently, as victims, we're all broken until God heals us in our own unique journeys."

Bloom in the Dark: True Stories of Hope and Redemption, made its debut in 2015, a year before Priz's book, Ditch the Drama. On their own unique journeys of healing, Priz and Wallace had no clue how their hearts for hurting women would lead them to work together.

Through the Christian Women in Media Association (CWIMA), God connected Wallace and Priz to each other and to Monica Schmelter, General Manager for WHTN (Christian Television Network's Nashville affiliate). After reading Bloom in the Dark, Schmelter asked Wallace to be a guest on her show, Bridges, which, in its nineteenth year, is available in over fifty million homes across the country every day.

With a bachelor's in communications, Priz, had already been interviewed on Nashville Alive, TCT's television show, when Schmelter also asked her to be a guest on Bridges. Having seen the talent and heart both Wallace and Priz showed on television through these interviews, Schmelter asked them to consider starting individual shows that would reflect their unique ministries: Bloom in the Dark, Inc. (a 501c3 charity) and Serenity Journey Ministries.

After much prayer and discussion, Priz and Wallace decided to work with Schmelter and WHTN channel 39, to produce Bloom Today as an extension of Bloom In The Dark, Inc. A weekly show, Bloom Today will air on Tuesday evenings at 9:30p.m. beginning July 4th.

When asked why the show is set in a kitchen with discussions happening around a bistro table, Wallace said, "I've always had my deepest conversations in my kitchen. That's where I've laughed, cried, and connected with my sisters and friends most often."

With episodes covering topics that are traditionally swept under the carpet rather than discussed on Christian TV, Bloom Today is unique in its blend of humor, pain, and healing. "When I give someone a hand (literally) on the show, or we celebrate a meaningful charity, or laugh with our current 'Ex-Victim of the Week', our intent is to have fun helping hurting women understand they are not alone. Hope and healing are available." Priz tells us. "We and our guests tell our deepest hurts, hidden brokenness, worst mistakes, and how we found hope and healing in a personal relationship with Christ."

"We go first in admitting the most shameful or embarrassing things so that the viewers will know they aren't alone. Our hope is that this will encourage others to be honest about their own stories and reach out to God and trusted family or friends to ask for help on their journey to healing. We wish churches were better at addressing these issues that are so rampant. God has heard the cry of hurting women everywhere and has asked us to reach them through this show." Priz continued. Wallace agreed. "Even though I didn't even have a TV in my house until I was 24, I recognize that television is the best way to reach hurting women where they are. In their bedrooms, kitchens, living rooms—in the safety of their own homes. Many don't recognize that I'm still a missionary even though my mission field is in American homes. Bloom Today is shining light in the darkest areas of brokenness and abuse so that we can see the realities of our situations and look to God for healing. It's never too late to ask God to heal us."

Priz and Wallace laughed as they told us that they end each show saying "use the fertilizer of your past to Bloom Today!"

Introduction
Best when watched with tissues and a box of chocolates.

PERSONAL USE:

We're so glad you are considering growing in your understanding of the broken side of the world and taking more steps in your own journey toward healing.

We recommend that you look through the topics of the coaching tools and choose the easiest one for you to watch first. This will be completely different for each person based on your specific journey and stage of healing. We also recommend that you only watch one per week. Give yourself time to process and pray about what's brought up by the episode and coaching tool. Don't rush. Ask God to reveal Himself to you in a new way through this time.

Give yourself grace. Be kind to yourself. We strongly recommend that you include a trusted friend on this journey if that's possible. If you're in counseling or seeing a professional right now, please discuss this with them prior to beginning. The discussions or tools may bring up painful memories from the past. Be prepared to reach out for help. We believe that "every trauma trigger is an opportunity to heal" when processed with appropriate help and support.

If you feel unprepared to handle any topic, do NOT proceed with that episode without the appropriate help and support. Please read "**DISCLAIMER**" below before proceeding.

To access the Bloom Today episodes, visit BloomTodayTV.com.

GROUP USE:

We recommend that this group be directed by a counselor or pastor with trauma training. Members of the group should be made aware of topics in advance so that they can skip a topic if they are not prepared to process that topic yet.

Leaders, if you are intending to use this for group viewing and discussion, be sure to let members know that they are free to leave if any of the material is triggering or overwhelming for them. Please provide options or referrals for professional counseling or intervention.

Please read "**DISCLAIMER**" before beginning your group's use of this tool. We also recommend that the leaders preview material so they can be prepared to handle possible issues and questions that may be raised.

To access the Bloom Today episodes, visit BloomTodayTV.com.

PROFESSIONAL USE:

We recommend that you preview all episodes before sharing with a client. Please read "**DISCLAIMER**" before proceeding. Each episode and coaching tool is independent and may be used by itself or in conjunction with others.

To access the Bloom Today episodes, visit BloomTodayTV.com.

Disclaimer

GINNY PRIZ AND PAULA MOSHER WALLACE ARE CERTIFIED LIFE COACHES, **NOT** COUNSELORS. THIS COACHING TOOL IS NOT INTENDED TO DIAGNOSE OR TREAT ANY MENTAL ILLNESS, TRAUMA, OR PTSD. WE RECOMMEND THAT THE ADVICE OF MENTAL HEALTH PROFESSIONALS SUPERCEDE ANY AND ALL STATEMENTS MADE IN THE EPISODES OR ON THE COACHING TOOLS. IF YOU EXPERIENCE ANY UNUSUAL THOUGHTS OR SYMPTOMS AS YOU INTERACT WITH THIS MATERIAL, PLEASE CONTACT A PROFESSIONAL IMMEDIATELY. EVERYONE HAS DIFFERENT LEVELS OF PAIN AND DAMAGE, CAUTION IS ADVISED IN THE USE OF THESE MATERIALS.

WE WORKED DILIGENTLY TO STAY TRUE TO SCRIPTURE AND GOD'S HEART ON EACH ISSUE. THIS BEING SAID, WE ARE NOT INFALLIBLE. WE RECOMMEND THAT YOU PRAY AND ASK GOD TO GIVE YOU DISCERNMENT ABOUT WHAT YOU HEAR. ULTIMATELY, YOU ARE RESPONSIBLE FOR YOUR CHOICE TO USE THESE MATERIALS AND WHAT YOU DO WITH THE RESULTING THOUGHTS AND EMOTIONS. WE'RE PRAYING THAT GOD COVER YOU WITH HIS LOVE AND WALK YOU FORWARD IN YOUR HEALING JOURNEY.

How God's Will Fits into a Broken World

Satan comes to steal, kill and destroy as many good things as possible. (John 10:10)	Vs.	Every good thing comes from God. (James 1:17)

Examples of What the Enemy Wants You to Think:

- Abuse and brokenness are God's punishment for sin.
- Because you are experiencing pain:
    - God must hate you
    - He forgot about you
    - You don't matter to Him
- That God is waiting for you to mess up and thinking up new ways to hurt you.

God's Truth Says:

God wants to love us.
- "For God so loved the world that He gave His only son so that whosoever believes in Him will not perish, but have eternal life." – John 3:16 (NIV)
- You are God's child. (John 1:12)
- You are Christ's friend. (John 15:15)
- He is not ashamed to call you brother. (Hebrews 2:11)

God wants to redeem us.
- "And we know that in all things God works for the good of those who love him, who have been called according to his purpose." Romans 8:28
- You have been redeemed and forgiven. The debt against you has been canceled. (Colossians 1:14)
- You have been rescued from the domain of Satan's rule and transferred to the kingdom of Christ. (Colossians. 1:13)

God wants to bless us.
- Jesus said "Which of you, if your son asks for bread, will give him a stone?" - Matthew 7:9 (NIV)
- You have been established, anointed, and sealed by God in Christ, and you have been given the Holy Spirit as a pledge guaranteeing your inheritance to come. (2 Corinthians 1:21; Ephesians. 1:13,14)
- You have been blessed with every spiritual blessing. (Ephesians 1:3)

Notes

Listen to This Song:

"The Voice of Truth" by Casting Crowns

Questions to Help You Process This Concept:

1. Have you ever believed any of the enemy's lies above? If so, who told you those lies?

2. If you truly believed in your heart that God wants to love, redeem, and bless you, how would you:

   a. See yourself differently?

   b. Treat yourself differently?

   c. Talk to yourself differently?

3. The things you think about the most will affect how you see your life and circumstances. Did you know you can choose to direct your thoughts toward God and away from the enemy's distraction? Or do you tend to let your mind wander based on the world and people around you?

Notes

4. How much time do you spend reflecting on the frustrations, losses, worries, and injustices you experience? How much time do you spend reflecting on God's blessings, promises, love, grace & mercy?

Exercises:

First, pray and ask God to help you with the exercises below.

1. This week, make an effort to guide your thoughts back to God's truth and correlating scriptures above.

   - God wants to love you
   - God wants to redeem you
   - God wants to bless you

2. Spend some journaling and listing all the ways God has blessed you, loved you, and shown His grace and mercy toward you.

I'm Not a Victim, am I?

DENIAL. Nothing really happened. Ignore the pain.	Vs.	Recognizing the brokenness and admitting to being a victim opens the door to healing

Examples of What the Enemy Wants You to Think:

- Technically, nothing really happened to you.
- It wasn't that bad. You are over reacting to the situation.
- You cannot trust your feelings – you're too emotional.
- If you speak up, people will only blame you and judge you.

Defining a Victim:

You were harmed or hurt as a result.
- If anyone has used their power, influence, authority, or relationship to do you harm or to hurt you, then you are a victim (regardless of how many times it happened, how severe it was, or what relationship that person has to you).
- If you are hurting as a result of the behavior of others, you are a victim (motivation is not the determining factor, the resulting pain is).
- If you are hurt as a result of your own behavior, you are a victim of yourself (self-hatred and addictions can make you a victim of your own dysfunction).

The threat of being harmed can cause you harm.
- Fear is the primary weapon in the control/abuse game.
- The threat of harm is as powerful as the harm, especially if it has been done previously (If you've been punched in the face once, the threat of the punch causes harm).
- Restricting access to freedom causes all other threats to have more impact (take away money, transportation, and other avenues of escape and the victim is at the mercy of the abuser psychologically).

Watching someone else being harmed can cause you harm.
- Fear of being harmed in the way you've seen someone else get harmed will keep a victim afraid and controlled.
- The brain's response to the trauma of viewing brutality is similar to the damage of the actual trauma.
- Once you know that someone is capable of abusive behavior, it is normal to be afraid that the harm may be done directly to you.

Notes

God's Truth Says:

Admitting you are a victim doesn't label you for life. Your identity is still firmly rooted in Christ. Your value does not diminish by owning the reality of what has happened to you.

When you admit to being a victim, you can ask God to begin the healing process so that the damage doesn't fester under the surface of denial. Like cancer, only a diagnosis and treatment will keep it from killing you over time.

Become an Ex-Victim:

- Admit you've been a victim.
- Ask God to start your healing journey with you.
- Be humble enough to ask for help.
- Ask God to give you a supportive team to help you.
- Do what God asks you to do on this new journey to heal.

This way you can become an Ex-Victim who shares hope and healing with others.

Watch This Video:

"Audio Book Teaser" by Bloom In The Dark

Questions to Help You Process This Concept:

1. Have you ever been physically harmed, threatened, or been witness to violence? If so, what effect did it have on you?

2. Have you ever been left hurting as a result of someone else's words, accusations, or lies? Have you hurt yourself by repeatedly criticizing and/or devaluing your behavior or reactions?

Notes

3. Emotional abuse can be harder to identify due to it being a result of manipulation, many times by a narcissist. If you feel someone in your life has the power to yank you around emotionally, consider researching emotional abuse in any of the Christian resources available online.

4. Has anyone been sexually inappropriate with you? Have they touched you without your approval? Did they proceed to force sexual intimacy on you after you said no or pulled away? Did they imply through words or actions that they could force you to have sexual contact of any kind against your will? Have they verbally harassed you with suggestive sexual talk or requests?

5. Has anyone used God or the Bible to control you or do you harm? Have they coerced or manipulated you to do things against your will because of a "religious" rule or scripture? Has the "submit" scripture been used to control your actions or behaviors?

Notes

6. If you have answered yes to any of these questions, please consider getting help through a counselor, recovery program, pastor, or trusted friend. At least research any areas you feel might be a part of your story that might be doing you harm. Awareness is the first step toward health and healing.

But I'm Not Beautiful

Beauty is on the outside, determined by culture and trends.	Vs.	Beauty is on the inside, determined by God based on the purity of our hearts.

Examples of What the Enemy Wants You to Think:

- God made me ugly.
- I'll never be as beautiful as _____.
- I need to fix my nose, hair, weight, skin color, wrinkles, etc.
- God wasn't fair in how He created me.
- I lost my beauty, so now I'm worthless or unworthy.

God's Truth Says:

"The Lord does not look at the things people look at. People look at the outward appearance, but the Lord looks at the heart." – 1 Samuel 16:7b (NIV)

God sees past our DNA.
- Every culture in history has a different standard of beauty. It is ever changing over time.
- Every creature was made by God. He took the time to craft each one of us in detail, not as an afterthought, but as a masterpiece.
- God's creativity knows no bounds. The shapes, colors, and varieties of species He created are anything but cookie-cutter! What makes us different, makes us beautiful!

God sees past our performance.
- God's creativity extends into our personalities - beyond our physical bodies. Introverts, extroverts, introverted extroverts, and extroverted introverts are all His creations!
- He's called all of us to be authentic about whom He created us to be, regardless of our hair style, what kind of clothes we wear, what job we hold, how much money we make, etc.
- Integrity and character matter to God more than our appearance, job description, or ethnicity.

Notes

God sees the heart.
- "If I give all I possess to the poor and give over my body to hardship that I may boast, but do not have love, I gain nothing." - 1 Corinthians 13:3 (NIV)
- God doesn't care about what you *look* like you're doing. He values the posture of your heart.
- If we are seeking God's heart, then we will see the fruit of the Holy Spirit in our lives: love, joy, peace, forbearance, kindness, goodness, faithfulness, gentleness, and self-control.

Watch This Video:

"Wonderfully Made" by Ellie Holcomb

Questions to Help You Process This Concept:

1. Have you ever felt ugly? What criteria did you base this on?

2. Have you ever compared yourself to others based on appearance? To whom? In what ways?

3. Have you felt like God wasn't fair in how He designed you? In what ways?

Notes

4. Have you felt a loss in value based on changes in physical appearance? In what ways?

5. "God saw all that He had made, and, behold, it was very good." - Genesis 1:31 (KJV) Have you ever thanked God for how He made you? Or have you been ungrateful?

6. What do you think it would feel like to see yourself the way God sees you? He sees us clothed in His righteousness and washed whiter than snow (Look up Isaiah 1:18, Isaiah 61:10, and Psalm 132:9)

Exercises:

1. Pray for God to show you how He sees you.

2. Make a list of positive character traits you see in yourself in the following areas. If you have trouble, ask a trusted friend to share the positive attributes they see in you.

3. Make a list of negative character traits. Ask God to help you become willing to repent of these, ask His forgiveness, and choose to become more like His son instead.

4. Ask God's forgiveness for any way you have rejected how He created you.

I'm Married, so it can't be Abuse, Right?

Abuse - power & control over the other person	Vs.	Marriage vows - love & honor each other

Examples of What the Enemy Wants You to Think:

- You must submit to your husband even if he is doing you harm.
- Marriage is more important than your life or wellbeing.
- You are a failure and disgrace if you get divorced.
- Your kids need you to stay together even if it is training them that abuse is normal.

God's Truth Says:

Marriage represents balance.
- Wives are to submit to their husbands so that husbands can lift them up, protect them, and love them (not to give husband's permission to harm their wives).
- "Husbands, love your wives, just as Christ loved the church and gave himself up for her." - Ephesians 5:25 (NIV)

Marriage represents teamwork.
- Marriage was never intended to give control; it has always been meant to represent God's heart for the church.
- While each person in a marriage has distinct roles, neither one is better or worse than the other. They are meant to work together so both can be filled up by the Holy Spirit and have life to the full.
- "Now that I, your Lord and Teacher, have washed your feet, you also should wash one another's feet. I have set you an example that you should do as I have done for you." - John 13:14-15 (NIV)

Marriage demonstrates God's perfect love.
- God's heart is to love and protect, never manipulate, control, or abuse.
- "Be completely humble and gentle; be patient, bearing with one another in love. Make every effort to keep the unity of the Spirit through the bond of peace." - Ephesians 4:2-3 (NIV)
- Codependence is not healthy, even in marriage. Each person's value needs to be found in Christ and not tied to anyone else's opinions or expectations.

Notes

Watch This Video:

"Hey Girl" by Nicole C. Mullen

Questions to Help You Process This Concept:

1. Have you ever felt someone had the right to control you because of their relationship with you? (family member, parent, spouse, etc.)

2. Have you ever believed your thoughts or opinions were more/less important than anyone else's?

3. Have you felt like staying married was more important than your safety or wellbeing? (We're not advocating divorce because you're just not "happy" or "fulfilled" by your spouse. We're speaking specifically to situations where they are doing you harm.)

4. Has the fear of being publicly shamed by divorce prevented you from admitting you're in an abusive marriage?

Notes

5. Read Ephesians 5:25-33. What does this tell you about God's intention for marriage symbolizing His relationship with the church?

6. Have you ever considered that each person's role within marriage was intended to draw us closer to God and understand mutual sacrificial love?

7. Has marriage become your idol rather than seeking and trusting God?

Exercises:

1. Pray about whether or not you're demonstrating Christ's love to your spouse.

2. Make a list of any ways your spouse has done you harm (physically, sexually, verbally, emotionally).

3. If you have questions about the safety of your marriage, find a Christian counselor that can help you get clarity on the reality of your situation.

Reclaiming Lost Dreams After Hardship

Give up on your dreams.	Vs.	There is another way or time God wants to fulfill His dreams for me.

Examples of What the Enemy Wants You to Think:

- Your dreams will never be fulfilled.
- Accept defeat.
- Stop trying to think you're better than you really are.
- God doesn't want you to be happy.
- God is punishing you by closing doors and removing opportunities.

God's Truth Says:

Reevaluate
- Is this God's will for me?
- Sometimes, we choose a different path than the one God has designed for us, so He closes doors to get us to come back to His plan.
- God's plan is always better for our eternal best because He sees all of the challenges and triumphs we will face in the future.

Reconsider
- Is there another way to go after this dream?
- Sometimes God asks us to pray about HOW to pursue the dream. We may have to ask Him for creative ideas or ask others for help rather than forging ahead.
- Stumbling blocks can become stepping stones, but you don't want them to be stepping-stones if you're going in the wrong direction.

Restructure
- Is there a change I need to make in my plans?
- If you put your dreams on the altar, God can resurrect them or give you new ones.
- Perhaps God is not saying "no" but rather "not yet."

Watch This Video:

"Just Keep Livin'" by McKenna Hydrick

Notes

Questions to Help You Process This Concept:

1. Be honest about your internal motivations. Is the heart behind your dreams to give God glory or have you ignored His plan in favor of how you imagine your dreams should come true?

2. Instead of waiting on His timing, are you looking for a shortcut or the easy way?

3. If your path is not lining up with your expectations, are you asking God to change your expectations? There is peace when our expectations line up with His.

4. Jesus said, "Not my will, but Yours be done." Do you want God's best for you more than you want your own will?

Notes

5. Manipulation can many times get us what we want. This can have long term consequences (Abraham had Ishmael because he manipulated an answer instead of waiting for God to give him Isaac). Are you trying to manipulate answers to a problem rather than trusting God to provide?

Exercises:

1. Ask God to show you if you have moved ahead of His will in favor of convenience, fear, or worldly gain.

2. If you have gone ahead of God, repent and ask forgiveness for running ahead of Him.

3. Ask God to show you His best for you.

Am I Still Lovable After Failing?

No one will love me because I messed up.	Vs.	Nothing can separate me from the love of God.

Examples of What the Enemy Wants You to Think:

- You don't deserve love.
- This sin is unforgivable.
- Who will ever love you now?
- No one will ever respect you again.
- You knew better, so it's your fault. You deserve to be rejected.
- This sin will follow you around for the rest of your life.

God's Truth Says:

Perfect love casts out all fear of rejection.
- When we accept the truth that God's love is unconditional, we can rest in knowing that no matter what people may say or think, we are still wanted and valued by the creator of the universe.
- God is love.
- God loves us unconditionally.
- "For I am convinced that neither death nor life, neither angels or demons, neither the present nor the future, nor any powers, neither height nor depth, nor anything else in creation, will be able to separate us from the love of God that is in Christ Jesus our Lord." - Romans 8:38-39 (NIV)
- "There is no fear in love; but perfect love casteth out fear: because fear hath torment..." - 1 John 4:18 (KJV)

Fear has consequences.
- Physical consequences: anxiety and stress can affect our bodies negatively and manifest in illness, high blood pressure, etc.
- Future consequences: When we trust God, He often asks us to step outside our comfort zone to love others. We receive a peace from the Holy Spirit that we are walking in God's will. But when we make decisions out of fear, we often shrink back in an attempt to protect ourselves. It can result in harmful isolation, feeling stuck or stifled, and increases our attachment to fear.

Notes

- "Thou wilt keep him in perfect peace, whose mind is stayed on thee: because he trusteth in thee." - Isaiah 26:3 (KJV)

God can heal and restore anything.
- God can restore our broken relationships, broken heart, or crushed spirit if we will give Him the opportunity.
- But this means we will need to get out of His way and only move when the Holy Spirit tells us to move. If we try to fix the broken things of this world by ourselves, we will often only make a bigger mess.
- "Trust in the Lord with all your heart and lean not on your own understanding; in all your ways submit to Him and He will make your paths straight." - Proverbs 3:5-6 (NIV)

Watch This Video:

"His Eye Is on The Sparrow" by Lauren Hill & Tanya Blount

Questions to Help You Process This Concept:

1. The Bible is full of examples of great men who have committed great sins. David was an adulterer, Moses was a murderer, and Jonah ran away from God. They each felt undeserving of God's favor afterward, but God still used them. What have you done that left you feeling unredeemable or undeserving of love?

2. How does it make you feel to know that no sin is too big for God to stop loving you?

Notes

3. What hurting place in your heart or broken relationship do you need to stop trying to fix and trust God to come in and heal?

4. Where have you been walking by sight and not by faith? What steps can you take to start walking by faith?

5. What decisions have you made out of fear rather than trusting and obeying the Holy Spirit? Have they left you feeling God's peace or more fearful?

Notes

Exercises:

1. Ask God to show you where you have been walking by sight and not by faith.

2. Repent of trying to control God's plan or other people. Repent of any area you have been running away from the Holy Spirit's prompting in fear.

3. List each situation or hurt you need to give to God.

4. Ask the Holy Spirit to reveal to you what steps you can take (or need to stop taking) that will help you live by faith rather than sight. Stepping out (or holding back) in faith can feel scary, but remember that God can be trusted to work in all things for our good.

Do I Deserve Forgiveness?

I can't forgive myself because I don't deserve it.	Vs.	We do not deserve forgiveness, but God forgives us anyway when we repent because Jesus died for our sins.

Examples of What the Enemy Wants You to Think:

- I chose that sin so I don't qualify for forgiveness.
- God might forgive me, but I just can't forgive myself.
- What I did was too horrible.
- But I knew better.
- I was already a Christian when I committed this sin.

God's Truth Says:

Jesus died on the cross for all our sins.
- Some sins we commit out of habit, instinct, or gut reaction. Others we take the time to choose even though we know it is against God's will. No matter how we committed them, Jesus already died for them.
- "Come now, let us settle the matter," says the LORD. "Though your sins are like scarlet, they shall be as white as snow; though they are red as crimson, they shall be like wool." – Isaiah 1:18 (NIV)
- "For as high as the heavens are above the earth, so great is his love for those who fear him; as far as the east is from the west, so far has he removed our transgressions from us." – Psalm 103:11-12 (NIV)

Satan causes shame and guilt but the Holy Spirit gives the gift of repentance.
- Satan is the accuser that brings thoughts and feelings meant to torment us with shame and guilt.
- The Holy Spirit convicts with the gift of repentance, which always includes His heart of hope and redemption.

Choose to forgive yourself.
- We have a choice to believe Satan's lies and stay in bondage, or step out of our shame and fully accept God's forgiveness.
- Repent to God and to yourself for the sin (even if you deliberately chose the sin).
- Accept your forgiveness that came at the incredible cost of the Son of God dying.
- Give yourself that same compassion and forgiveness.

Notes

Poem:

Hope Blossoms
By Angela Washington

Trouble used to be like weeds,
sprouting up without seeds.
But the God I serve and love,
sent a blessing from above.
Now, there's hope in each flower,
and a blessing every hour.
I can run from end to end,
knowing God forgave my sin.

Questions to Help You Process This Concept:

1. Is there anything in your past or present that you are still feeling guilt or shame over?

2. Have you repented of that sinful habit, decision, or reaction? Repentance is not only feeling sorry for your sins, it is also taking responsibility and then changing or turning around in your attitude and behaviors. Repentance includes making different decisions to remove the habit, avoiding temptations, and choosing to seek to understand God's heart.

3. If you've repented, have you truly accepted God's forgiveness? Even when your emotions may not line up, are you verbalizing your acceptance of God's forgiveness?

Notes

4. Jesus died for ALL your sins. Are you forgiving yourself for those sins? If not, do you realize that you've been saying you're better than God? He forgives you. Truly accepting His forgiveness means forgiving yourself.

Exercises:

1. Make a list of areas that you still feel shame and guilt over.

2. Repent to God for each sin on the list.

3. Say out loud, "I accept God's forgiveness for _____" for each sin.

4. Then, say out loud, "I forgive myself for _____" for each sin.

5. To symbolize destroying the bondage of guilt and shame that comes through not forgiving yourself, permanently destroy that list.

What If I Was Abandoned?

You were abandoned because you're not loveable	Vs.	God will never leave you nor forsake you, and nothing can separate you from His love.

Examples of What the Enemy Wants You to Think:

- I'm not worth loving.
- If I were loveable, they would have stayed.
- There must be something wrong with me.
- It's my fault that they left.
- What I did makes me unlovable.
- I was born unlovable so no one will EVER love me.
- I'm worthless, so they threw me away.
- Because this person abandoned me, I'll never be loved by anyone.

God's Truth Says:

He will never leave you.
- If you are abandoned as a child, it is not a reflection of you or your behavior. It is a reflection of their issues or problems.
- Many times our core beliefs about God are reflective of our own broken experiences with our earthly father or parental figure(s). (For example, if you've been abandoned by a parent, then you may believe God will abandon you as well)
- Feeling abandoned can often times open the door to fear of experiencing abandonment again from anyone, anywhere. As a coping mechanism, you may become overly attached to others or overly detached from others.
- "Be strong and courageous. Do not be afraid or terrified because of them, for the Lord your God goes with you; **he will never leave you nor forsake you**." – Deuteronomy 31:6 & Hebrews 13:5 (NIV, emphasis added)

Nothing can separate us from His love.
- God's love for you is not dependent on your performance. He will continue to love you because you are His child without conditions.
- "Whoever does not love does not know God, because God is love." – 1 John 4:8 (NIV)
- God created us to need His love, and no human love or connection will fill that need.
- "Neither height nor depth, nor anything else in all creation, will be able to separate us from the love of God that is in Christ Jesus our Lord." -Romans 8:39 (NIV)

Notes

God is the Father to the fatherless.
- Scripture tells us that God wove us together in our mother's womb. He has had a vested interest in bringing us to this world from our very beginning.
- God adopts anyone who believes in His Son as their Savior into His kingdom family as His child.
- Just because you are not a child anymore, doesn't mean you do not need God to be your father just as deeply as when you were a child.
- "A father to the fatherless, a defender of widows, is God in his holy dwelling." - Psalm 68:5

Watch This Video:
"Good Good Father" by Chris Tomlin

Questions to Help You Process This Concept:

1. Do you have difficult building healthy relationships due to loss or abandonment in your childhood?

2. If you were abandoned as a child, do you feel like it is your fault? Is there something stopping you from recognizing the adult's fault in the situation?

3. Many times, we can seek healing from this kind of wound by trying to heal the original broken relationship, or seek a new relationship to replace it. Have you done this? How or with whom?

Notes

4. In realizing how other people's brokenness affects us, have you ever considered that the person who abandoned you had been hurt or abandoned in their past?

5. Have you been able to forgive the person who abandoned you? If you have, your identity and value will no longer be tied to this loss?

Exercises:

1. Find five scriptures that describe God's love for you. Since His word is truth, you can trust that these scriptures are more real than your feelings.

2. Memorize these scriptures and place them in prominent places where you can see them and be reminded of them throughout the day.

3. Make a list of the people who have abandoned you in some way. Remember, God has never left you or forsaken you even if you felt like He did.

4. Pray for each person on the list and give them to God.

5. Take the time to feel and grieve the loss you experienced. There is no set time limit for this process, so do not be afraid if it takes a while. Even when it hurts, continue to feel and process rather than getting stuck or shutting down. Healing will come during and out of this process! (If you have a trusted friend that can walk with you through this, then ask them to support and pray for you. If not, ask God to walk you through it.)

6. Ask God to show you the ways He has been there for you.

Is There Grace After My Adultery?

You are condemned to live under shame and guilt without hope of love or trust from anyone.	Vs.	God will convict you of your sin so you can repent and draw closer to Him so He can redeem you from your sin and make you a new creation who is loved and free.

Examples of What the Enemy Wants You to Think:

- I deserve to be shunned and disgraced.
- I have committed an unforgivable sin.
- I'm an untrustworthy whore.
- I've destroyed my marriage and my family's lives.
- No one will love me ever again.
- I'm not worthy of forgiveness, so I can't forgive myself.

God's Truth Says:

Do I want to run away from God or toward God?
- If you are wrapped up believing the enemy's lies, then you are bound to want to hide from God in fear or shame or guilt (like Adam and Eve did).
- But God wants us to come to Him, *especially* after we have sinned. This allows Him to deal with us gently. He desires to show us where we tried to live on our own power and did not trust Him. This is what makes us susceptible to temptation.
- God wants to show us how to heal by standing on His truths that build us up and restore us.
- Always run toward God rather than away from Him: "Do you not know that in a race all the runners run, but only one gets the prize? Run in such a way as to get the prize...we do it to get a crown that will last forever." - 1 Corinthians 9:24-25 (NIV)

Do I just accept blame or do I want to take responsibility and repent?
- Repentance turns us around to go toward God. Jesus paid for this gift of repentance by dying on the cross. Because the price has been paid for our sins, God only asks that we change our hearts to accept responsibility and move in a new direction – toward Him.
- "If we confess our sins, he is faithful and just and will forgive us our sins and purify us from all unrighteousness." - 1 John 1:9 (NIV)

Notes

- While we do need to change some of our routines and behaviors as a part of repentance, repentance is not just about our actions. God is more concerned with the state of our heart and our desire to love and trust Him. Ultimately, it is about restoring our relationship with a loving God.

Do I feel ashamed or hopeful?
- Shame and guilt are rooted in fear, whereas hope is rooted in God's love.
- When you reach out to God with the full truth of what you have done, you'll find that He will still love you. He wants you to bring Him into the cracked and hurting places of your heart. He is love, and love casts out the shame and guilt rooted in fear.
- As long as God has given you breath, He is not done writing you into His story. Trust His lead. Let Him show you how He wants to work with you to strengthen His kingdom.
- "Many are saying of me, "God will not deliver him." But you, LORD, are a shield around me, my glory, the One who lifts my head high." - Psalm 3:2-3 (NIV)

Watch This Video:

"Still That Girl" by Britt Nicole

Questions to Help You Process This Concept:

1. Ask yourself the three questions above to help you determine where you are. Have you been living under Satan's condemnation or God's conviction?

2. Which of the enemy's lies mentioned above do you believe or struggle to resist? Are there any more that were not on this list?

3. Have you been running away from God or toward God with your thoughts and feelings? If you've been running away, what has held you back?

Notes

4. How do you think it would it feel if you brought all of your junk and pain to God and He loved you and forgave you anyway?

5. Are you sensing that something is interfering with your relationship with God? Could it be shame or guilt? If so, repent so that you can be restored to His loving heart.

Exercises:

1. Make a list of any areas of sin that you still feel shame or guilt about.

2. Take that list to God in prayer and confess. (If you have a trusted friend, ask them to walk through this with you.)

3. Ask God to forgive you and then choose to forgive yourself.

4. Ask God to be merciful and cancel any curses associated with the sins.

5. Ask God for healing and restoration in any areas that the sin has consequences.

Following God When It's Not Fair

You shouldn't have to do the right thing if others didn't. That wouldn't be fair.	Vs.	God holds each of us accountable to follow Him regardless of whether or not it is fair or expected by others.

Examples of What the Enemy Wants You to Think:

- He didn't do what he should, so I don't have to do what I should.
- That wasn't fair, so I'm not going to _____.
- They didn't repent, so I don't have to forgive.
- No one does that because it's not fair.
- Everyone is a hypocrite, so I'm not going to pretend by doing the "Godly" thing.
- It's not fair that I'm supposed to obey God when no one around me is.
- It's not fair because this is tough, painful, or hard.
- Why me?

God's Truth Says:

Love God.
- Loving God means obeying Him. It's not just a feeling, it's an action that will result in a deeper relationship with more feelings of love.
- "If you love me, keep my commands."- John 14:15 (NIV)
- Jesus paid the ultimate unfair price by dying for us when we were still sinners. Who are we to demand "fair" circumstances in order to be obedient?
- "'Love the Lord your God with all your heart and with all your soul and with all your mind.' This is the first and greatest commandment. And the second is like it: 'Love your neighbor as yourself.' All the Law and the Prophets hang on these two commandments." - Matthew 22:37-40 (NIV)

Love your enemies.
- The second most important command is to love our neighbor as ourselves—this includes our enemies.
- Even when God tells us to love our enemies, it's for our own good. Hate is destructive.
- "Love your enemies, do good to those who hate you, bless those who curse you, pray for those who mistreat you." - Luke 6:27-28 (NIV)
- We can be in deeper, loving relationships with God and others when we're loving everyone.

Notes

Forgive others.

- You can't love someone if you're bitter against them. Forgiving God, yourself, and others for all perceived wrongs will open the door to love.
- Forgiveness also sets you free. It's not about the other person getting away with what they've done, it's about you not paying the price for their sins in your own prison of bitterness and anger.
- "For if you forgive other people when they sin against you, your heavenly Father will also forgive you. But if you do not forgive others their sins, your Father will not forgive your sins." - Matthew 6:14-15 (NIV)
- God offers forgiveness for our sins, but He absolutely requires that we forgive others. It's not optional. (It also doesn't mean that you need to be in fellowship if that person is doing you harm. You can forgive and love without being in fellowship.)

Watch This Video:

"Forgiveness" by Matthew West

Questions to Help You Process This Concept:

1. Have you ever directly disobeyed God because it seemed He was asking something unfair? When?

2. Have you chosen to obey God despite unfairness and then felt closer to Him? When?

3. Have you ever felt closer to God after forgiving someone? Was it fair that you had to forgive in that situation?

Notes

4. Ultimately, what is more important to you: being right with God or life being fair? Why?

5. Has obeying God and putting Him first brought good fruit into your life through added freedom, love or joy? Are there areas where you want more freedom, love or joy? (Reaping these fruits in one area of obedience to God will bear fruit in other areas as well.)

Exercises:

1. What has God asked you to do in obedience that you haven't wanted to do because it wasn't fair? Make a list.

2. Repent for not obeying in each area.

3. Choose to obey God as a sacrifice of love to Him, regardless of anyone else's choices or the unfairness of the situation.

4. Make a plan for actually following through in each situation. (God honors each baby step in the right direction.)

5. Ask a trusted friend to help you and hold you accountable.

Can God Use Satan's Evil for Good?

If you're damaged in any way, Satan has won in that area permanently.	Vs.	God can restore you regardless of what harm Satan has done because God loves you and has paid the price to redeem you.

Examples of What the Enemy Wants You to Think:

- I'm damaged goods, so no one will ever want me.
- I'm worthless because my parents didn't love me.
- I deserve the abuse because everyone abuses me.
- God must not love me because humans hurt me.
- Give up, I'm a lost cause.
- I've failed one too many times.
- I don't deserve a normal life.
- I'll never be better off than I am now.
- No one loves me.
- God's promises are only for other people.
- How could anyone ever love me?

God's Truth Says:

Satan is a liar and the father of lies.
- Satan only influences you when you believe him.
- Satan's lies come to us in the form of thoughts, other's words, or inherited beliefs.
- Scripture is a great antidote to these lies (when not taken out of context).
- "When he lies, he speaks his native language, for he is a liar and the father of lies." - John 8:44b (NIV)

We were purchased by Christ's sacrifice so He could redeem us from the curse of sin.
- Satan lost his ability to determine our futures when Jesus died on the cross to redeem us from our sins.
- Jesus bought us with a price, the blood of Jesus Christ. (1 Corinthians 6:20)
- "Christ redeemed us from the curse of the law by becoming a curse for us...He redeemed us in order that ... by faith we might receive the promise of the Spirit." - Galatians 3:13-15 (NIV)

Notes

Jesus made a final purchase if we believe in Him and accept his adoption.

- "He predestined us for adoption to sonship through Jesus Christ, in accordance with his pleasure and will." - Ephesians 1:5 (NIV)
- Satan got access to us through sin so he could torment us in our spirits, souls, and bodies, but he lost those rights when Jesus died on the cross for our sins and Father God adopted us into His family.
- "Now if we are children, then we are heirs—heirs of God and co-heirs with Christ, if indeed we share in his sufferings in order that we may also share in his glory." - Romans 8:17 (NIV)

Watch This Video:

"I Am Yours" by Jimmy Needham

Questions to Help You Process This Concept:

1. What destructive beliefs have you accepted as true? Even when scripture says otherwise?

2. Satan does harm through other people's choices so that he can persuade us we are hopeless. Who has hurt you in a way that feels like permanent damage?

3. Are there areas of sin or brokenness in your life that you believe permanently separate you from God's love or healing? What are they?

Notes

4. Have you found a trusted pastor, counselor or mentor who can help you identify lies that are holding you back from healing? Who could you talk to about your hidden damage?

5. Have you started believing you are truly a child of God with all the love and belonging that you are entitled to? If not, why not?

Exercises:

1. Read scriptures on the next page before answering these questions.

2. Ask a trusted friend to walk you through this exercise.

3. What areas of your life feel hopeless or worthless? (Identify specifics.)

4. Ask God to help you add to this list from your past and childhood.

5. For every negative you wrote down, find at least one scripture in the list on the next page that speaks God's truth into that situation.

Notes

He accepts you:
- I am God's child (John 1:12)
- I am Christ's friend (John 15:15)
- I have been bought with a price; I am not my own; I belong to God (1 Corinthians 6:19,20)
- I have been established, anointed and sealed by God in Christ, and I have been given the Holy Spirit as a pledge guaranteeing my inheritance to come (2 Corinthians 1:21; Ephesians 1:13,14)
- I have been redeemed and forgiven. The debt against me has been canceled (Colossians 1:14)
- I am hidden with Christ in God (Colossians 3:3)
- I have been saved and set apart according to God's doing (2 Timothy 1:9; Titus 3:5)
- He is not ashamed to call me brother (Hebrews 2:11)
- I am a member of Christ's body (1 Corinthians 12:27; Ephesians 5:30)
- I am an heir of God since I am a child of God (Galations 4:6,7)

He has made you secure:
- I am a citizen of heaven, seated in heaven right now (Philippians 3:20; Ephesians 2:6)
- I am free forever from condemnation (Romans 8:1)
- I have been blessed with every spiritual blessing (Ephesians 1:3)
- I may approach God with boldness, freedom and confidence (Ephesians 3:12)
- I have been rescued from the domain of Satan's rule and transferred to the kingdom of Christ (Colossians 1:13)
- I am firmly rooted in Christ and am now being built in Him (Colossians 2:7)

He has made you significant:
- I am a saint (Ephesians 1:1; 1 Corinthians 1:2; Philippians 1:1; Colossians 1:2)
- I am the salt of the earth (Matthew 5:13)
- I am the light of the world (Matthew 5:14)
- I am part of the true vine, a channel of Christ's life (John 15:1,5)
- I am chosen by Christ to bear His fruit (John 15:16)
- I was chosen in Christ before the foundation of the world to be holy (Ephesians 1:4)
- I am a minister of reconciliation (2 Corinthians 5:17-20)
- I have the right to come boldly before the throne of God to find mercy and grace in time of need (Hebrews 4:16)

Why Are You Better Than Me?

You're worse than everyone else. Or You're better than everyone else.	Vs.	We are all equally valuable as God's children created for unique roles in the Kingdom.

Examples of What the Enemy Wants You to Think:

- I'm not enough _____.
- I'm too much _____.
- I'll never be like them, I should just stop trying.
- God made a mistake with me.
- I'm not smart, pretty, tall, skinny, or _____ enough.
- At least I'm smarter, prettier, taller, skinnier, or _____ than _____.
- It's not fair that they get to _____, and I don't.
- It's not fair this horrible _____ didn't happen to them, but it did to me.
- If only I could be, have or do more.
- At least I'm not as messed up as they are.
- I went through worse and didn't turn out as bad as they did.

God's Truth Says:

He created you specifically.

- Each person was made by God intentionally to be different. It is impossible to accurately compare even two. It would be as if comparing apples with roller coasters.
- Each fingerprint is unique as God's reminder that we're not meant to be clones.
- God put you together to be YOU.
- "For you created my inmost being;...and your works are wonderful I know that full well." - Psalm 139:13-14 (NIV)

He prepared a plan for you specifically.
- Even siblings in the same family can have vastly different interests. One sibling may be a doctor while another is an artist. Neither is better because God wanted both.
- The paths God prepared for us are as unique as our makeup. Comparing our journey to others was never what God intended. Satan will use it to bring pride or discouragement (Luke 18:11).
- If we compare ourselves or our mission to anyone, it should be to Jesus – the only

Notes

person without sin. Not to condemn our current path, but to convict us and encourage us to be more like Him.

- We are created to play a specific role in the body of Christ, we all need each other to function in a healthy way. God gives more honor to the parts that seem to get less honor. (I Corinthians 12:12-27)
- "For we are God's handiwork, created in Christ Jesus to do good works, which God prepared in advance for us to do." - Ephesians 2:10 (NIV)

He executes His plan for you specifically.

- Joseph's path to becoming second in command of the reigning world power was very different from Daniel's rise in a world power.
- God opens doors and allows trials to teach us the lessons that we specifically need and to grow the skills where we are specifically lacking to do His will and be complete.
- "He leads me in the paths of righteousness for His name's sake." - Psalm 23:3 (NKJV)

Watch This Video:

"Unbreakable" by Jennifer McGill

Questions to Help You Process This Concept:

1. Have you ever asked God to show you His purpose in how He designed you? If not, ask Him.

2. Who do you feel is better than you? Who do you think you are better than? Why?

3. How has comparison stopped you from doing something you know God wanted you to do?

Notes

4. Have you been comparing your weaknesses to others' strengths? (For example, comparing your real life to a social media highlight reel?)

5. Have you found your place in the body of Christ? Are you fulfilling your specific calling to God's glory?

Exercises:

Exercise 1:
1. Think of ways that you've seen yourself as more than or less than others.

2. Write them down in two columns:
   a. "more than" (I am better than others in these ways – I have two hands and Ginny only has one)
   b. "less than" (I am worse than others in these ways – I have only two hands but Ginny has a choice of removable hands and hooks)

3. Look at the first person or item on your list. Recognize that this comparison is not truth. Cross it out and replace it with one of the following 3 truths that best applies:
   a. God created me uniquely
   b. God has a specific plan for my life
   c. God executes His plan for me specifically

4. Repeat step 3 for all of the people/items on both lists.

Exercise 2:
1. Next, ask God to show you how He made you unique. Write down each positive, unique trait on a sheet of paper, then add the unique plan you see in your story. (Ask a trusted friend what they see in you if you have a hard time.)

2. Review your list of traits. Thank God for each way God created you uniquely and has worked in your life through your story.

Even a Princess Considered Suicide

You have no hope so you might as well end it all.	Vs.	God always has a plan for you so trust Him even in the "valley of the shadow of death" where He will guide and comfort you if you ask Him to.

Examples of What the Enemy Wants You to Think:

- The world will be better off without me.
- No one will even notice if I'm gone.
- The people I love will be better off without me.
- Suicide is the only way to end the pain.
- No one can live through this type of pain.
- They'll be happier without me ruining their lives.
- I can't do this anymore.
- I can't handle the rest of my life hurting this much.
- Ending my life is the only way to get out of this situation.

NOTE: THE EXAMPLES ABOVE ARE ALL LIES!!! The enemy feeds us these lies that "feel" like truth in the darkness and pain. (*If you are fantasizing suicide, get help immediately. Call a suicide hotline 1-800-273-8255, a pastor, counselor, or 911. Your life is worth saving. No matter what you currently think or feel.*)

God's Truth Says:

We find purpose in our pain.
- Although we may not be able to recognize it at the time, God is working in even the hardest times for our good. If we can turn to Him in the midst of that pain, we will eventually be able to see how He orchestrated our lives to never waste a hurt.
- When we seek to build muscle, we know we must break down that muscle and experience soreness and pain as it rebuilds stronger. Similarly, pain can build our faith muscles stronger than ever when we cling to God and His truth and promises in the hardest of times.
- "Not only so, but we also glory in our sufferings, because we know that suffering produces perseverance; perseverance, character; and character, hope. And hope does not put us to shame, because God's love has been poured out into our hearts through the Holy Spirit, who has been given to us." – Romans 5:3-5 (NIV)

Notes

We can trust God with our futures.
- "Being confident of this very thing, that He who has begun a good work in you will complete it until the day of Jesus Christ;" – Philippians 1:6 (NKJV)
- God has a plan to for your future. He wants you to bring Him into your life and into your pain so He can walk arm-in-arm with you, spreading hope for His kingdom.
- It has been said that our greatest passion comes from our greatest hurt. And while God does not desire for us to be hurt, He does desire to redeem and use the pain of this broken world.
- By making decisions based on a belief that His promises are true, we start to walk by faith, and not by sight. We are limited in what we can see and understand, but God is not limited and can see all the days of our lives.

Christ's death signifies our value.
- "For you are bought with a price: therefore glorify God in your body, and in your spirit, which are God's." - 1 Corinthians 6:20 (NIV)
- Jesus died on the cross so that God the Father, Son, and Holy Spirit would never have to be separated from you for eternity. He wants to know you and be close to you THAT BADLY.
- He has not done this to leave you in a world where there is pain, but to include you in a new world and heaven that is coming where every tear is washed away permanently.

Watch This Video:

"Who You Are: A Message To All Women" by Jon Jorgenson or
"Who You Are: A Message To All Men" by Jon Jorgenson

Questions to Help You Process This Concept:

1. *If you are actually fantasizing suicide, get help immediately. Call a suicide hotline 1-800-273-8255, a pastor, counselor, or 911. Your life is worth saving. (No matter what you currently think.)*

2. Do you see yourself as a beautiful child of God? If not, ask Him to show you how He sees you. (He paid for you with His life, so Jesus definitely values you as priceless!)

Notes

3. Have you been focusing on today? This hour? This moment? Trusting God to carry you through the next five minutes? (There is a time for everything, even a time to cry and feel pain, but it is not forever. Trust God with today and give Him all of your tomorrows.)

4. Suicide is a temptation that needs to be faced with help. Are you being honest with a trusted person about this temptation? (Shining light on this darkness can help us survive this season without permanent consequences. We recommend getting professional help if at all possible during this season.)

5. Are you surrounding yourself with encouragement and support? Who and what around you feed you life and hope?

6. Are you listening to worship and positive music exclusively? Are you reading and watching entertainment that feeds life rather than death? (Feeding the soul with life rather than validating darkness through what you see and hear.)

7. Are you exercising in any way? (Exercise of some type can help your body produce positive hormones that can help you see your circumstances from a more hopeful place. This isn't about losing weight or body image. This is about using your body's natural processes to improve your feelings. Exercise also helps your body detox and release stress.)

Notes

Exercises:

1. Look around you. Do the things around you make you feel good or bad? Is there any way to remove the things that make you feel bad?

2. What music are you listening to? Commit to listening to nothing but positive, non-triggering music for a month. How does that change how you feel?

3. What entertainment are you feeding yourself? Is it feeding hope in your life, or making you hurt worse? Choose only life-giving entertainment for a month. Does that change how you feel?

4. Are the people you spend time with encouraging you or hurting you more? Choose to spend more time with encouraging people and less (or none) with toxic people who drag you down.

5. *If you are actually fantasizing suicide, get help immediately. Call a suicide hotline 1-800-273-8255, a pastor, counselor, or 911. For more resources, hotlines, and charities go to www.bloominthedark.org/resources*

Is Addiction the Root of My Problem?

You're an addict and you'll always be an addict who is surrounded by drama and conflict no matter what you try.	Vs.	God made you whole and provides everything you need to be at peace. The chaos in you and in the world, like addiction, is a result of us believing the enemy and his lies.

Examples of What the Enemy Wants You to Think:

- I'm the problem, here. It's all my fault.
- What is wrong with me?
- There must be something wrong with me since everyone doesn't struggle the way I do.
- Why can't I do better? Try harder? Have more willpower?
- I'm a useless addict. Why should I even try to change?
- No matter what I do, I always screw things up.
- Why doesn't anyone really love me?

God's Truth Says:

Stop the insanity.
- Addiction is an important problem that can be life-threatening. We encourage _anyone_ struggling with _any_ addiction to please seek help from a counselor, anonymous twelve-step group, or other support group in your area. It is important to treat the addiction with proven tools and facilities as needed for your safety and health.
- However, addiction is not the true root of the issue. There are some deep-seeded lies that the enemy has encouraged you to believe from your early years. To escape the pain of those lies or fill your need for love, you have turned to addiction – consciously or unconsciously.
- Satan wants to keep distracting all of us from the real problem. He would rather have us running around stomping out the symptoms (lack of willpower, conflict, drama, incarceration, etc.) instead of dealing with the core issue (guilt and shame from abuse, believing you're broken, unlovable, not good enough, worthless, etc.).
- The enemy wants us working on ourselves just enough to keep us busy, but not enough to address the true roots of the issue and actually access our true freedom in the love of Christ!
- If we stay just below the surface, we will only make more work for ourselves by attempting to deal with the symptoms. We will go in circles and waste precious time

Notes

and energy we could be putting into a relationship with God and working for His Kingdom.

- The woman at the well had four husbands and was living with a fifth man. She was ashamed to show her face in public until she finally met Jesus and believed He would give her eternal life despite all the mistakes and bad choices she had made. After He addressed the root lie of being worthless and unlovable, the woman not only lost her shame, but sought out the people of the town to tell them about Jesus, with her head held high! (John 4)

Start true healing.

- "He heals the brokenhearted and binds up their wounds." - Psalm 147:3 (NIV)
- Whether you are just starting your recovery journey, or you've been in recovery for years, it's important to face and deal with the actual problem: hurts of your past and the need to be loved.
- This is often the place you'd rather not look. You'd rather run or stuff it down or ignore it, but this tactic is not any less difficult or painful. When you clean out an old infected wound, the pain you feel is a productive, necessary pain to experience true and *lasting* healing as an overcomer.
- Choose to get out of denial and stay out of denial. This is a choice, and you can take pro-active steps to confront the lies and rationalizations.

Find clarity and peace.

- "The thief comes only to steal and kill and destroy; I have come that they may have life and have it in abundance." - John 10:10 (CSB)
- When Satan's lies are revealed, you are free to welcome God's truth into your heart and come closer to Him than you've ever been before.
- Finally rest in being loved by God. He is the "lover of your soul" who "never leaves nor forsakes you."
- As you walk in your recovery and healing, always reach out to others to help them along the way. This way we experience God's love by giving and receiving it.
- Discover your path to help others to feel the purpose and fulfillment found in sharing God's love.

Notes

Reflect on this painting:

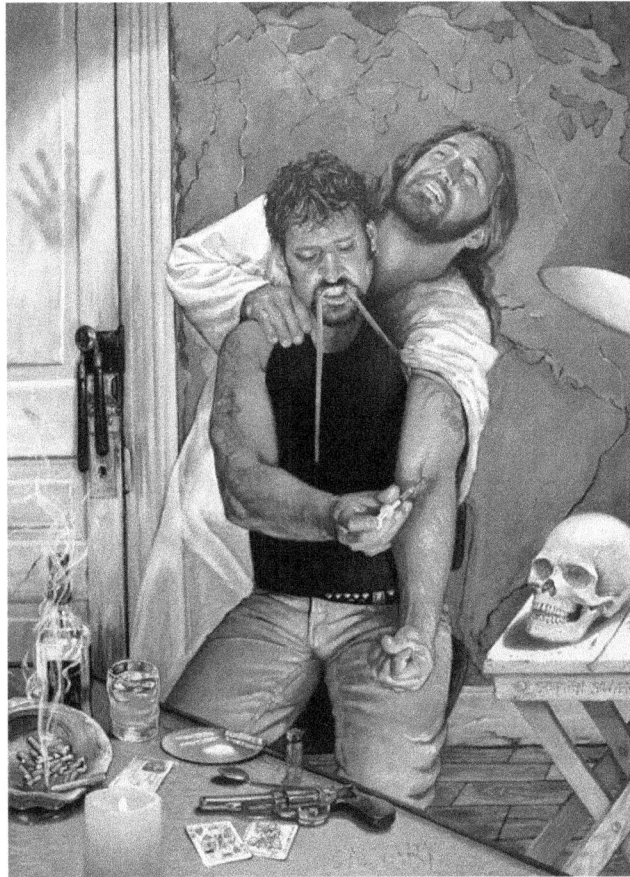

Title: "Calvary" By: Stephen Sawyer
You can order a print of this at www.art4god.com/store/Calvary1

Questions to Help You Process This Concept:

1. Do you ever feel a hollow place inside that you want to fill? What do you want to fill it with?

2. Are there areas or people in your life that you want to run away from? Where do you run to?

Notes

3. Do you have areas of pain or discomfort that you want to avoid? What do you choose to do instead?

4. Have others complained that you do something too much? Or teased you for "always" doing something? What are those "somethings?"

5. Identifying your "go to" actions or substances can help you identify areas of addiction. Then look at the times you choose those actions or substances. Whatever caused you to want to fill or avoid is pointing to the real problems. Are you willing to start facing those?

Exercises:

1. If you are ready to look below the surface, the first step is to get connected to a recovery group, counselor, and/or sponsor to support you throughout the process.

2. Identify the situations that cause you to have an extreme reaction (see above).

3. Bring these reactions to God and ask Him to show you where you were first hurt in this area.

Notes

4. If you are not sure what thoughts or feelings you are experiencing in these highly charged moments, ask God to help you identify them. You can also see a counselor to help you decipher your thoughts and feelings.

5. Unraveling the mess of addictions and their roots is a messy, complicated process for most. Give yourself grace. Ask God to direct you to a safe person who can help you get the help you need. That's what we did.

From Rape to Nascar Chaplain
(Having A Need to Fill A Need)

I should do whatever it takes to feel better and hide the pain.	Vs.	Only God can actually heal the internal brokenness to help us have lasting freedom and joy.

Examples of What the Enemy Wants You to Think:

- It's better to hide my hurt instead of letting it out for the world to see.
- I'm ashamed to let anyone know what happened.
- Pretending it didn't happen will make it all go away.
- This drink, high, porn, purchase, fantasy, Netflix, or cake will make it all feel better.
- I can forget about the pain if I have enough distraction.
- This distraction worked to take away the pain before, it should work again.
- I'm entitled to be angry because what was done to me can never be undone.
- Besides, escape is way better than acting out my anger and hate.

God's Truth Says:

Addictions just dull or numb pain temporarily.
- Substances and distractions cannot heal the root issue, and the pain always returns.
- Coming to God with your pain and letting Him heal you from the inside will require a process of surrender, feeling, forgiveness, and service. But once God has walked you through the process, the original wound will be completely healed. You will no longer have a need to cover, minimize, or distract from it.
- "For everything in the world--the lust of the flesh, the lust of the eyes, and the pride of life--comes not from the Father but from the world." – 1 John 2:16

Addictions only create the illusion of feeling safe or in control.
- Denial tells us we can stop any time we want to. But we still refuse to stop.
- You may have a specific benchmark for what defines an "addict" that exempts your behavior as "addicted." If you're obsessing in your mind about drinking, drugs, shopping, etc. that is a more accurate gauge.
- Addictions can give a temporary illusion of control/safety that never lasts past the "high" or "escape."
- The reality is you are powerless over 99% of life. This is a hard reality to come to terms with, especially since we like to create a sense of order around us. But this is the reality.

Notes

- Even though we are powerless, God is still on the throne. We can feel safe knowing God is in control.
- We win this war one day at a time by surrendering to God here on earth, so that our ultimate victory will be experiencing eternity in heaven.
- "Whoever loves money never has enough; whoever loves wealth is never satisfied with their income. This too is meaningless." – Ecclesiastes 5:10 (NIV)

Addictions may provide escape from circumstances but not from yourself
- When we look to worldly things to satisfy our anxiety, fear, pain, anger, or discomfort, we are always ultimately left to deal with ourselves. "Wherever you go there you are."
- God gives peace in the midst of the storm. We can stay calm knowing we have God as our strength and shield, while everyone around us changes and freaks out.
- "It is better to heed the rebuke of a wise person than to listen to the song of fools." – Ecclesiastes 7:5 (NIV)

Watch This Video:

"What Faith Can Do" by Kutless

Questions to Help You Process This Concept:

1. Do you run from your pain, anger or circumstances and to any specific substance or activity?

2. Would you rather stew in your anger, than feel the fear, pain or rejection that is behind the anger?

Notes

3. Are you rationalizing that feeling the pain or anger won't do any good?

4. Do you think that the preferred escape is actually less destructive than facing the pain? Why do you think that?

5. Is there anything that you obsess about in your mind and need to hide that is keeping you from being authentic/transparent in your relationships? Have you considered that it may be an addiction?

Exercises:

1. Follow the steps below to address the pain and anger you are trying to cover up or run from.

2. Get in a safe, quiet place where you will not be disturbed for at least 20 minutes. Take several deep breaths and get into a comfortable position.

3. Prayer this prayer:
   Heavenly Father, I know You see all of me and love me still. Thank You for loving me despite my flaws and sins. Help me to bring my thoughts and emotions into the light so You may heal me from the pain I am trying to hide. I ask that You silence any self-depreciating thoughts that arise as I examine my emotions. Place Your peace on me. Allow me to accept my emotions without judgment. Open my eyes so that I might see myself as You see me.
   In Jesus' name I pray, Amen.

Notes

4. Continue to breathe deeply. Imagine the tension in your muscles being exhaled with each breath. With your eyes closed, pay attention to how your body feels. Notice your head and neck, your shoulders, chest, arms, back, stomach, hips, legs, feet. Relax each muscle group as best you can.

5. Before you move ahead, remember, you are in a safe place and emotions are a symptom. They are something you have and not a permanent part of you.

6. Once you are relaxed, consciously allow an emotion to rise up to the surface.

7. Imagine you are holding it in your hand. Examine how it feels and where you feel it in your body. Just observe, knowing it will not overpower you.
   (If you want to cry, go ahead and cry. If you want to scream or smash something I suggest you imagine doing so in your mind. As uncomfortable as the emotion may be, take some time to sit with it (continue deep breathing) and monitor its intensity.) As you feel it without judgment, you'll find the less intense it becomes.

8. Can you identify the emotion you are feeling?

9. Do you know where and when it came from?

10. Finally, imagine releasing the emotion to God. It has done its job: to alert you to a thought that needs addressing. It may not go easily, and it may come back, but for this moment, release the emotion to the Lord.

If you feel that this process has been outside of your capability, consider walking it through with a counselor, sponsor, pastor, or mentor.

Looking for Love in All the Wrong Places

You need someone to choose to love you in order to validate your worthiness and lovability.	Vs.	A close relationship with God fills and satisfies the deep need for unconditional love in our hearts that no human can.

Examples of What the Enemy Wants You to Think:

- If I can't make this relationship work, I must be a failure. There must be something wrong with me, at least.
- What's the point of life if I can't share it with someone?
- It's not the same loving God because He can't physically hold me.
- God said it's not good for man to be alone, so He wants me to find a partner.
- I can't do life on my own.
- It's impossible to be happy and confident without someone loving me the way I want.
- I'm incomplete without a partner.
- If only I would find my soul mate, I'd be okay.

God's Truth Says:

Treat yourself as God would treat you.
- God treats each of His children with respect and care because He loves them so deeply. It is the broken people of this world that cannot provide the unconditional love that our heart is looking for.
- Treat yourself as the temple of the Holy Spirit so you can begin to see your value with Him at your center.
- Discover your true value which is ONLY found in Christ.
- Leviticus 19:18 says "Love your neighbor as yourself." If you're not loving yourself, then you have nothing to give your neighbor.

Teach others to treat you as God would.
- "Do not give what is holy to the dogs; nor cast your pearls before swine lest they trample them under their feet, and turn and tear you to pieces." - Matthew 7:6 (NKJV)
- We teach others by the behavior we accept. If we don't value ourselves, others are less likely to see our value.
- By accepting disrespect, we are approving it and sometimes even encouraging it.

Notes

- If they respect you, they will stay around. If they don't, they will leave when you don't accept that disrespect.

Foster deeper, balanced relationships.
- The steps above sift out the people who are around for the wrong reasons. The people who are left are generally capable of having healthier relationships.
- Like attracts like. Be the person you want to be surrounded by.
- You are free to be yourself in those relationships. There is no need to be fake or hide your flaws with those who love and respect you without ulterior motives.
- "Make no friendship with a man given to anger, nor go with a wrathful man." - Proverbs 22:24 (ESV)

Listen to This Song:

"In The Eye of the Storm" by Tammy Daniel

Questions to Help You Process This Concept:

1. Have you ever put your need for human love above your relationship with God?

2. Have you ever listened for God's promptings to choose your friends and romantic relationships? Or do you move forward on your own based on your gut feelings? Why?

Notes

3. If you were asked to describe the perfect friend or romantic partner, would you list physical attributes and shared hobbies? Or would you focus on their relationship with Christ, their character, and/or their ability to treat you with kindness and respect?

4. How much time or effort do you put toward finding or keeping the perfect friend or romantic partner? How much quality time do you spend getting to know God and building a relationship with Him? Which has taken priority in your life?

5. How much time do you spend carefully weighing the character traits of a potential partner before you let your guard down? If their character is questionable, are you comfortable building a boundary or do you entertain those who show an interest in you?

Exercises:

Exercise 1:
1. Reflect on the ways you have treated your time, body, money, values, and emotions. List any ways you have not treated them with care and respect the same way you would another person's.

2. Consider how you could make space to protect these things in your life. It is not selfish to protect what is important to you.

Notes

Exercise 2:

1. Reflect on the way others have treated you (friends and romantic relationships). Have they treated your time, body, money, values, and emotions with care and respect?

2. Consider educating others on how you wish to be treated with respect. If they continue to disrespect you, how could you hold your boundaries to protect these areas in your life? It is also healthy to put space between yourself and those who have repeatedly disrespected you in any combination of these areas.

Exercise 3:

1. Third, consider those people in your life who have repeatedly encouraged you, respected you, spoke the truth in love (not condescension), and listened without judging. These are your quality, safe people.

2. If you do not have a physical person like this in your life, remember that God the Father, Jesus, and the Holy Spirit are always there for you to listen, speak truth in love, encourage, and respect you. Pray that God would lead you to recognize these people and help you bring them closer into your life.

3. If you do have people like this in your life, reach out to them and communicate your appreciation for their care and respect.

I'll Be the First in My Family

This broken behavior is just how you are because it's how your family has always been.	Vs.	With God's help, you can break any family pattern or curse, because you are a new creation in Christ Jesus.

Examples of What the Enemy Wants You to Think:

- I am doomed to relive my family's dysfunction.
- There isn't anything special about me that I could break out of the mold.
- I just have bad genes.
- It's too hard to change when I'm the only one who wants to, or who sees the value.
- I'm scared of being judged and ridiculed for changing.
- What if I fail? It's better not to try than look like a failure or a hypocrite.

God's Truth Says:

Recognize the pattern.
- When we are raised to think or behave a certain way, in some areas it can be difficult to see where our thoughts or actions do not align with God's word. Others are very apparent, because we despised how the behavior harmed us growing up.
- You can spot patterns by examining your family behavior and comparing and contrasting it to the families of your friends, neighbors, or somewhat realistic healthier television families (This Is Us, Full House, etc.)
- "Always learning and never able to come to the knowledge of the truth." – 2 Timothy 3:7 (NKJV)

Break the pattern.
- It may be too difficult to change patterns using your own strength. Do not be ashamed or too hard on yourself if this is the case. These are often ingrained patterns of thinking and behavior that started before you spoke your first word or attended elementary school. There may even be spiritual influences passed down from your previous generations (Deuteronomy 28)
- We have the Holy Spirit, a champion who wants to help and guide us, along the path to change. Asking for the help of the Holy Spirit is not a sign of weakness, but of great faith and trust in the Lord's power. He wants to work with you.

Notes

- One of the most powerful steps to change is intentional, heartfelt repentance. Not just being sorry for what you have done, but owning your sin, confessing it to God, and changing your actions out of love and genuinely desired obedience to the Lord.
- "But if they will confess their sins and the sins of their ancestors—their unfaithfulness and their hostility toward me,...I will remember my covenant with Jacob, Isaac, and Abraham." – Leviticus 26:40-42 (NIV)

Create a new pattern.
- New patterns are often difficult to create, but not impossible. We have to intentionally fight against all those instincts we used to follow.
- Although we are changing physically, this fight begins and ends in the spiritual realm. The effort we put in will have long-lasting effects not just on our own lives, but on the lives of our children and the lives of those around us.
- By identifying in which circumstances we want to change, we can pause before we react without thinking by asking God to come in and help us choose better responses.
- To help us make different choices, we can look in God's word for characters with similar struggles or glean wisdom from the book of Proverbs. We can also ask God to reveal His character to us through His word, so that we can strengthen our relationship with Him and thereby strengthen our desire to walk in His will. This is how we can use the Bible to renew our minds from our old ways of thinking, to embracing the truth.
- "Therefore, if anyone is in Christ, he is a new creation; old things have passed away; behold, all things have become new." – 2 Corinthians 5:17 (NKJV)

Listen To This Song:

"The Curse Is Broken" by James Fortune

Questions to Help You Process This Concept:

1. Are there any behavior or thought patterns you'd like to change in your life right now? Make a list.

Notes

2. What are the family secrets, values, or behaviors that may have influenced you toward these unhealthy or sinful behaviors?

3. In what areas have you blamed your upbringing or family history for sinful or unhealthy behavior?

4. Have you ever tried to change this behavior? If so, what did you find difficult or easy about the process? If not, why?

5. Have you ever reverted back to old sinful or harmful behavior where you had previously seen successful change? If so, how did you bring God into the change? How did you ignore Him during the reversion?

Notes

Exercises:

1. Pray and ask God to show you any family patterns that He would like you to break free from. Make a list of the patterns you are aware of, or that God has revealed to you.

2. Reflect on Biblical characters that may have struggled with similar patterns (i.e. Jonah refused to follow God's call, Sarah who doubted and ran ahead of God's timetable, Moses was a murderer, David was an adulterer and murderer) or who showed how to avoid the patterns you are struggling with (i.e. David & Goliath, Jesus' temptation in the wilderness, Elijah & the Widow, Paul's ability to have joy despite his circumstances).

3. Take responsibility for your previous sin and repent. The Lord forgives completely those who repent.

4. Identify which people or circumstances might cause you to automatically revert to old patterns.

5. Create a plan to intentionally slow down, pray periodically before and during those circumstances.

6. Make a list of better choices you could make in each circumstance instead of the old, harmful ones.

7. Ask a trusted accountability partner to hold you accountable to the changes you are making.

Almost Beaten to Death for God
(God Never Wastes A Hurt)

You should despair in your broken-ness because it makes you worth-less and unlovable.	Vs.	God can change your story and use any and all of your hurt for His glory and to help others.

Examples Of What The Enemy Wants You To Think:

- I might as well just give up because I am too broken to help anyone.
- I'm damaged goods.
- Redemption is for everyone except me.
- My story is too _____ to be of any use to God.
- I'm just a screw up.
- Who would ever listen to me after what I've done?
- The fertilizer in my past is WAY too toxic and deep!

God's Truth Says:

God redeems the past.
- We can ask God to come into our story and redeem our past at any time.
- If we let God into the hurting places to heal those areas, we find pain is a catalyst to healing rather than the end of the story.
- Instead of despising the loss, we often become grateful for the lessons it taught us and our ability to help others in those areas.
- "For the sake of Christ, then, I am content with weaknesses, insults, hardships, persecutions, and calamities, for when I am weak, then I am strong." - 2 Corinthians 12:10 (ESV)

God brings victory over the enemy.
- Healing means we can move on from the pain of the past and do not need to be chained down to it.
- Because of Jesus' sacrifice on the cross, you're not a powerless victim of the enemy any more.
- Your faith and obedience to God empowers you to walk in God's plan for your life.
- "For just as we share abundantly in the suffering of Christ, so also our comfort abounds through Christ." - 2 Corinthians 1:5 (NIV)

Notes

God's brings hope through you.

- God's redemption and victory in your life brings hope to others.
- God's healing is never JUST for you. It is also to shine a brighter light in the darkness.
- You can always bring your wisdom forward to those who are still hurting in the dark.
- Helping others find healing and freedom is a simple way to redeem your past and help you stay free in your future.
- Genesis 50:20 makes it clear that people may intend evil, but God can still do good, including the saving of many lives.

Listen to This Song:

"Blessings" by Laura Story

Questions to Help You Process This Concept:

1. Have you felt like your brokenness disqualified you from helping others? How?

2. Do you believe your brokenness is too messy or ugly to be healed? Do you feel like you deserve ongoing consequences? (When Christ died on the cross, he took ALL our sins on Himself so we could truly be free.)

3. Have you asked God to heal you and then open your eyes for ways you can help others? When?

Notes

4. How has God used your pain or brokenness (even in small ways) to give hope or help to someone else?

5. Have you let go of shame or guilt in your past? Is there any you are still holding onto? Make a list.

Exercises:

1. Make a list of your hurts on a piece of paper.

2. Ask God to heal you in these areas of hurt.

3. Take the list and draw a cross over the list.

4. Ask God to show you how to use your story of pain to encourage someone else.

A Trauma Triggered Avalanche

Every trauma trigger proves I'm defective and unlovable.	Vs.	Every trauma trigger is an opportunity to find deeper healing in Christ.

Examples Of What The Enemy Wants You To Think:

- I am a lost cause, no one will ever love me.
- This just proves I'm actually insane.
- There's something wrong with who I am because I overreact.
- My situation is hopeless.
- There's no point in living because of this.
- This problem or situation has completely destroyed my life.
- Others can handle this fine, I must be defective.
- It's everyone else's fault, I'll always be a victim.

God's Truth Says:

Victims need extra compassion and support.
- The enemy wants victims and supporters to be frustrated by confusion and drama.
- Victims may need extra help seeing the way out of the hopelessness and depth of damage triggered by a trauma.
- Complex trauma makes each damaging situation feel exponentially more destructive
- LOVE rather than judge or criticize—even when it's yourself you're evaluating.
- Blaming and shaming never brings healing.
- "Let us not become weary in doing good, for at the proper time we will reap a harvest if we do not give up." – Galatians 6:9 (NIV)

Victims need healing beyond the latest trauma.
- Old wounds are exacerbating current hurts. Overreacting to a current situation usually means there is deeper hurt that hasn't healed. For example, slapping an open wound hurts a LOT more than slapping a healthy area.
- Victims feel the old hurt plus the new hurt simultaneously. Extra prayer, kindness, love, and support will help the victim find hope sooner.
- PTSD may trigger an age and maturity discrepancy. If an adult situation triggers a trauma response, the victim may regress to the maturity level at which the first trauma in this area actually occurred. For example, a sexual attack on a thirty-five-year-old woman may trigger her to the eight-year-old she was the first time she was molested.

Notes

- Look for ways to add safety, love, and support to help the trauma victim find hope and healing. Rather than pointing out the brokenness, encourage them by telling them that they're not alone. Show love first and foremost.
- "Scorn has broken my heart and has left me helpless; I looked for sympathy, but there was none, for comforters, but I found none." – Psalm 69:20 (NIV)

Victims may need professional help.
- Help is available through counseling, Celebrate Recovery, other recovery programs, support groups, coaching, or medical professionals.
- Consider a trauma response as an opportunity to get help for underlying issues. Ask God to direct you in to a safe, effective option to begin processing previous damage.
- Not every option will be the right one for you. You may need to try different options before finding a good fit for you to be safe in processing your deepest hurts. No matter what, don't give up. Run to Christ for hope and healing rather than running away from the pain or feeling hopeless.
- "For just as we share abundantly in the sufferings of Christ, so also our comfort abounds through Christ." – 2 Corinthians 1:5 (NIV)

Watch This Video:

"Just Be Held" by Casting Crowns

Questions to Help You Process This Concept:

1. Have you ever felt like you way overreacted to a tough situation? Do you know why?

2. Have you ever judged someone (or yourself) for overreacting to a problem? If so, when? Can you think of a more compassionate way to have handled that situation?

Notes

3. Have you ever asked for professional help? Why or why not? Have you felt there was a stigma around asking for help?

4. Does asking for help make you feel like a failure? Do you think that "good Christians" should be strong enough to handle problems on their own? Do you feel like prayer should always be enough?

5. Is there an area in your life that you should consider asking for help? If so, what is it?

Exercises:

Exercise 1:

1. Do you know someone who overreacts to problems? Write their name down on a sheet of paper.

2. Ask God to help you see their situation from His perspective of love.

3. Make a list of ways you could show love and compassion to them.

4. Plan a time to actually follow through on something(s) from this list.

Notes

Exercise 2:

1. Write your name on another sheet of paper.

2. Ask God to help you see your own situation from His perspective of love.

3. Make a list of ways you could show love and compassion to yourself.

4. Plan a time to actually follow through on what you've written down.

Why I Chose the Adult Industry

You must earn your value by satisfying the expectations of others – especially men.	Vs.	You are intrinsically priceless because you are designed by God, chosen by God, and loved by God.

Examples of What the Enemy Wants You to Think:

- Men desire with their eyes, so I need to get validation through my appearance.
- If you've got it, flaunt it.
- You'll never get married if you don't show off your assets.
- Being desirable gives you power over men.
- Your beauty is your only value, so if you're not beautiful, you have nothing.
- Do whatever it takes to look pretty and get men's attention.
- There is no way to get a man without being sexual.

God's Truth Says:

You are chosen.
- "Even before He created the world, God loved us and **chose us** to be holy and flawless in His sight." - Ephesians 1:4 (NLT)
- Even before you lifted a finger, God chose you to be His beloved child. He didn't chose you based on looks, fashion, or how fit you are.
- You have never been a mistake.
- You have never been an afterthought. God has always been very intentional about making you, YOU!

You are loved.
- "Even before He created the world, **God loved us** and chose us to be holy and flawless in His sight." - Ephesians 1:4 (NLT)
- God doesn't reject you based on how many times you've rejected Him or chased after men.
- No matter what you've done, or what's been done to you, God is still standing with His arms wide open patiently waiting for you to run into them.

You are seen.
- "Even before He created the world, God loved us and chose us to be holy and flawless **in His sight**." - Ephesians 1:4 (NLT)

Notes

- God does not judge you based on your outward appearance; He sees who you really ARE on the inside—your being.
- "For man looks at the outward appearance but the Lord looks at the heart." – 1 Samuel 16:7b (NKJV)
- God takes an active interest in even the most minute details of your life. He sees your efforts and walks with you through all your pain and triumphs.

Listen to This Song:

"True Beauty" by Mandisa

Questions to Help You Process This Concept:

1. Have you ever felt like your value was in your appearance? How did you learn that?

2. When you dress to go out, are you looking at yourself through the eyes of objectification? Are you seeing just your body parts?

3. If you've been measuring your worth based on your appearance, how much value do you think you have? Are you truly happy with your appearance?

Notes

4. Have you ever seen yourself through the eyes of someone who truly loves you for who you are? Do they see you are more beautiful than you see yourself?

5. Have you asked God to help you see the ways He values you? Your beautiful spirit, character, and heart.

Exercise:

1. Make a list of things you believe about your appearance. What you like and what you don't like.

2. Now cross out each trait you wrote. The good and the bad.

3. On the back of that paper, write down every character trait, talent, and success you've had.

4. If you can't think of any/many, ask a few people who are safe and loving. Write down what they tell you.

5. Thank God for each inner beauty characteristic you have. Ask Him to keep showing you more "inner beauty" characteristics so you can see yourself through His eyes.

What's My Real Source of Pain?

As soon as you handle this next challenge, you'll be fine. You can't make this life all that much better.	Vs.	God will help you uncover the lies you believed as a result from pain in your past and help you find freedom.

Examples of What the Enemy Wants You to Think:

- There's no point in digging up the past. All it will bring is hurt and pain.
- If I look at all that hurt, I will go off the deep end, and I won't be able to control my feelings ever again.
- I've just got stress at work. That's why I'm hurting physically.
- As soon as _____ happens, then everything will be better.
- This one person in my life is really the problem. There's nothing wrong with me.
- I'm not homeless. I can keep a job. So nothing in my past could have been THAT bad.
- Other people say I should just get over it, so I'm going to pretend it's not a problem.

God's Truth Says:

Everyone can recognize that their source of pain goes further back than their circumstances by asking these three questions:

Have you experienced recurring health issues?
- Often when there is deep pain from your past, your mind downplays the impact in order to survive or avoid more pain. But the truth is, that pain and unrest does not go away. It has to go somewhere. Many times, it shows up in your health.
- Do you have a recurring health issue, pain, or condition? High blood pressure, allergies, ulcers, tendonitis, cancers and hundreds of other conditions have been proven to be directly related to stress levels.
- These stress levels often go beyond that of healthy adults in a demanding job. We can blame our circumstances, but most likely there is a deeper hurt from earlier in life that has affected the way we see ourselves, our relationship to God, and others.
- "For physical training is of some value, but godliness has value for all things, holding promise for both the present life and the life to come." – 1 Timothy 4:8 (NIV)
- By exploring the root causes of our fears and sins, we can heal from the damage caused by old lies and be free to align with God's heart.

Notes

Have you experienced a pattern of relational dysfunction?
- Have anger issues prevented you from having healthy discussions with your spouse, friends, or coworkers?
- Has fear prevented you from making close, healthy relationships?
- Have your obsessive or fearful thoughts prevented you from trusting others?
- Has depression put you in isolation and made you be unable to connect with others and enjoy their presence? (Clinical depression is a more complicated disease that requires professional physical, emotional, and spiritual intervention. If you suffer from clinical depression, searching for the root of your pain with a counselor, therapist, or psychiatrist will help you, but it is not the only treatment you will need. You may also need medical intervention during this process.)
- "For those who live according to the flesh set their minds on the things of the flesh, but those who live according to the Spirit set their minds on the things of the Spirit." – Romans 8:5 (ESV)
- When we are brave enough to examine our true feelings, they will tell us where we are aligned with God and where our thinking has been misguided by the enemy.

Have you experienced recurring career roadblocks?
- Recurring problems at work may be connected to past unresolved damage.
- Obsessive thinking about your career as the source of your value will twist your perspective and make you feel like a failure no matter how much success you have.
- Dysfunctional relationships in the workplace can cause career roadblocks that interfere with your ability to succeed in a career.
- You need to find your value in Christ and let Him facilitate your career.
- "I am the vine; you are the branches. Whoever abides in me and I in him, he it is that bears much fruit, for apart from me you can do nothing." – John 15:5 (ESV)

Listen to This Song:

"He Knows" by Jeremy Camp

Questions to Help You Process This Concept:

1. In which area above have you felt the greatest struggle – personal relationships, health issues, or career roadblocks?

Notes

2. Is there a person or event in your past that causes either extreme emotion or nagging unrest in your mind or heart?

3. Do you purposely avoid thinking of a specific place, person, or incident from your child-hood?

4. What are your fears about looking deeper? Do you fear your emotions or the events of the past?

5. Have you asked God to help you deal with the past and your emotions? If not, why? If so, how have you seen Him answer your prayer?

Exercises:

1. Do you have any health issues? Write them down. Are any of them stress related?

2. Do you have problems in relationships? Write them down. Is there a pattern with the types of people you have issues with?

Notes

3. Have you had career issues or hang ups? Write them down. Are there any patterns to what happened?

4. Are there any lies that these problems have in common? Is there fear, stress, anger, bitterness, insecurity, rejection or other broken areas that may have deeper roots? Ask God to show you and write these down.

5. Repent for being in agreement with these lies.

6. Ask God to take these areas of brokenness and give you His love and truth instead.

Can Abuse Feel Normal?

The enemy only wants to hurt, shame, and cause fear by any means or person available and then downplay the damage.	Vs.	God's love heals and restores so it's safe to recognize abuse and brokenness to find more love and freedom.

Examples of What the Enemy Wants You to Think:

- What I went through really wasn't that bad.
- Other people have had it worse.
- I didn't turn out all that messed up because I can hold a job and I'm not in jail.
- There's no point in feeling pain from the past if I'm doing ok.
- But they loved me so it couldn't be abuse.
- They were trying to help me so it couldn't be wrong.
- I should just be grateful it wasn't worse.
- Any pain or fear I feel must be my fault.

God's Truth Says:

Reevaluate your pain using these three questions:

Where did someone shame you?
- Shame: Seeing yourself or your actions as irredeemable, unsalvageable, or truly horrible. In extreme cases this can include taking on shame for actions done to you.
- If their actions, words or attitudes made you feel ashamed, something was wrong. Love will never cause shame.
- Shame is a symptom that something was wrong. If you were a child, it was never your fault so you shouldn't be carrying the abuser's shame or guilt.
- Ask a counselor or pastor you can trust to help you identify the source of the shame and help you work through it.

Where did someone hurt you?
- Being honest about the brokenness is the first step toward finding healing. Denial never healed anything.
- If you were hurt, was there an action, attitude, or words that caused the pain?
- If you were a child, it wasn't your fault. Can you put the responsibility where it should go?

Notes

Where were you afraid?

- Perfect love casts out fear; it doesn't cause it.
- Who were you afraid of? When did that fear start? Who did you feel the need to avoid or get away from?
- If they were inappropriate or abusive to you, it will cause you harm—even if they also tell you they love you.
- "There is no fear in love; but perfect love casteth out fear: because fear hath torment. He that feareth is not made perfect in love." – 1 John 4:18 (KJV)

Listen to This Song:

"Your Name Brings Healing to Me" by Planetshakers

Questions to Help You Process This Concept:

1. Where did someone shame you?

2. Did someone hurt you physically? Who and when? (The level of intensity or frequency does not matter.)

3. Did someone hurt you emotionally by picking on you, bullying you, disrespecting you?

4. If you were hurt, was there an action, attitude, or words that caused the pain?

Notes

5. Who did you feel uncomfortable or unsafe around? Who do you feel uncomfortable or unsafe around today?

Exercises:

1. Write a list of your favorite safe people.

2. Write a list of your uncomfortable or unsafe people.

3. Were you tempted to put some of the same people on both lists?

4. What criteria did you use to decide what list to put someone on?

5. If you're honest with yourself, do you need to change anything?

6. Now, ask a trusted friend, counselor, or pastor to review the list with you to see if you have any blind spots related to abuse in your past. If you do, get help processing so you can continue healing.

Do Strong Men Cry?

The enemy wants to steal the gift of emotions God gave us by having us shut down our emotions or having our emotions control us.	Vs.	God gave us emotions as gifts to help us process and respond appropriately to the people and events around us.

Examples of What the Enemy Wants You to Think:

- Emotions mean you are broken and weak.
- I can't let my weaknesses show or they will know I am a fraud.
- I don't want my emotions to be a burden on anyone else, so I will stuff them down.
- Emotions aren't safe so it's better not to feel anything.
- My emotions run my life because I have no say in them.
- Other people's actions control my emotions and ruin my life.
- I only feel pain, so I'll shut down all feelings.
- _____ is the only emotion I can feel safely.

God's Truth Says:

"Cast your burden on the Lord, And He shall sustain you;" – Psalm 55:22a (NKJV)

Be aware of the pain.
- Pain is a gauge for brokenness. Pain is a warning system to help us know there is a problem (physically and emotionally).
- Every trauma trigger is an opportunity to heal because it lets us know there is a problem we can get help and healing for.
- If you want to feel the positive emotions, you have to feel and process the painful emotions to make room for the positive emotions.
- "A time to weep and a time to laugh, a time to mourn and a time to dance," – Ecclesiastes 3:4 (NIV)

Be aware of the joy.
- Joy is not dependent on circumstances. It is an internal attitude of the heart founded in Christ.
- Numbness is like general anesthesia, it causes you to lose the good emotions (joy, peace, humor, excitement, hope, love) as well as the painful or negative ones (anger, fear, hate).
- "The joy of the Lord is your strength." – Nehemiah 8:10b (NIV)

Notes

Be aware of the hope.
- Hope is the belief that your future holds good (to expect with confidence).
- Trust in God gives hope.
- Healing includes healthy processing of all emotions.
- Even baby steps show us there is hope and can motivate us to keep moving forward.
- "And not only that, but we also glory in tribulations, knowing that tribulation produces perseverance; and perseverance, character; and character, hope." – Romans 5:3-4 (NKJV)

Listen to This Song:

"Healing Begins" by Tenth Avenue North

Questions to Help You Process This Concept:

1. Have you shut down emotions or stuffed them? Why?

2. What emotions were you trying to avoid?

3. Do you struggle to celebrate, feel joy, feel love, or feel peace?

Notes

4. Have you tried to avoid people or situations that made you feel emotions?

5. Have you ever been able to process emotions in a healthy way? What would it be like to feel the range of emotions without them controlling you?

Exercises:

1. Write a list of emotions you are comfortable with.

2. Write a list of emotions you try to avoid at all costs.

3. Pray and ask God to help you identify and process the emotions you'd rather avoid.

4. Write down a few names of people who you've seen process positive and negative emotions in a healthy way.

5. What do you think of those people? Do you see them as weak and stupid or stable and strong?

6. How did their processing of emotions differ from yours?

Stopping the Spin Cycle

The enemy wants you to believe you have to be doing and performing to earn love and value.	Vs.	You can be still and trust God because your value is found in Him.

Examples of What the Enemy Wants You to Think:

- If you're not accomplishing things, then you're not worth anything.
- I'm only worth something if I'm taking care of other people.
- If anyone sees my flaws, then they'll know I'm not worth anything.
- I have to make sure others like me in order to know I'm worthy of love.
- If I can just fix this hurting person, I'll earn more of God's love.
- If I just did more, I'd be worth more.
- It's always my responsibility to help friends or family in need.
- If I don't do it, no one else will.
- If I'm not saving the world God won't love me.

God's Truth Says:

God gives you strength.
- God's strength to endure trials is given freely and does not require a deposit or exchange of effort in return. We can lean on Him every moment.
- God's gives His strength in more ways than one. When we are physically weak, He can give us strength to increase our faith and hope.
- "But they that wait upon the Lord Shall renew their strength." – Isaiah 40:31a (KJV)

God gives you protection.
- "The Lord will fight for you; you need only to be still." – Exodus 14:14 (NIV)
- Protection comes in the form of physical, emotional, and spiritual.
- As we walk through life, it is important to be constantly asking God where we are to step next and when. If we step out ahead of him, we could be jumping out of the path of safety He has set up for us.

God gives you blessings.
- "Remember the Sabbath day, to keep it holy." – Exodus 20:8 (KJV)
- There are any number of blessings God can orchestrate as a result of honoring the Sabbath as we are commanded:
    - o   We can receive the experience of hearing from God.
    - o   Our hearts can be mended by experiencing gratitude.

Notes

o   We can find afterward we are more focused and efficient.
o   Relaxation can reduce stress and chance of illness.
- Significant growth in our faith and relationship with Christ can come as a result of a season of waiting.
- Not every pain we see needs to be mended or fixed immediately. When we fix for others without asking God what He wants us to do, we may be stepping in and preventing another blessing.

Listen to This Song:

"Rest In Me" by Todd Vaters

Questions to Help You Process This Concept:

1. When was the last time you were truly still and waited on God?

2. Do you struggle with being still? Why or why not?

3. Which one of the lies above do you resonate with the most? Is there a lie about stillness you've internalized that is not on the list?

Notes

4. What do you surround yourself with that encourages and inspires you (artwork, scripture, etc.)? If you do not have any visual encouragement, what could you surround yourself with?

5. What kind of music do you listen to? Does it inspire you and quiet your mind or is it more likely to drag you down?

Exercises:

1. For the next five days spend quiet time with God.

2. Set a timer for thirty minutes.

3. Listen to one or two worship songs to usher in the Holy Spirit.

4. Spend the remainder of your time being still and listening to God.

What Choice Do I Have?

What I'm attracted to defines who I am.	Vs.	My true identity is found in who God created me to be.

Examples of What the Enemy Wants You to Think:

- God wanted me to be gay.
- If I have these thoughts, then it must be because this is who I am.
- It feels good so it can't be wrong.
- My happiness is more important than God's truth.
- My introduction to sexuality was by the same gender and I liked it, so that must be who I am.
- I am aroused by the same sex and not the opposite sex, so this is who I am.

God's Truth Says:

Choosing to live by God's truth brings:

Peace
- "The mind governed by the flesh is death, but the mind governed by the Spirit is life and peace." – Romans 8:6 (NIV)
- When we seek to find peace through physical means, we will always be left wanting. We can rest in who we were made to be in Christ Jesus.
- The world will always have many differing opinions about our behaviors. If we seek to live by them, we will continue to be exhausted and hurting.
- God has the truth that lasts throughout time. His word does not waver on the definition of sin. Even when we don't like it, we do not have to question where the line is drawn.
- "Or don't you know that he who unites himself with a prostitute is one with her in body? For it is said, "The two will become one flesh." But he who unites himself with the Lord is one with Him in spirit. Flee from sexual immorality." – 1 Corinthians 6:16-18a (BSB)

Beauty
- Recognizing we were made in God's image helps us see His beauty in us.
- God's design in nature and family relationships reveals to us His love and character. When we commit sexual sin, we are showing God we do not trust His design.

Notes

- "I praise you because I am fearfully and wonderfully made; your works are wonderful, I know that full well." Psalm 139:14 (NIV)

Fulfillment
- "For we are God's handiwork, created in Christ Jesus to do good works, which God prepared in advance for us to do." – Ephesians 2:10 (NIV)
- God wants to work with us. This life a journey we were meant to take together.
- Choosing to follow His commands will not always look or feel easy, but it will bring us deeper fulfillment than physical pleasure ever could.

Listen to This Song:

"Hard Love" by NEEDTOBREATHE

Questions to Help You Process This Concept:

1. What role, if any, has God played in your sexual decisions?

2. Which of the lies listed above have you believed in the past, or struggle with today?

3. Do you see any difference between sexual sin committed by a heterosexual person vs. a homosexual? For example, the Bible says that a husband cheating on his wife is sin just as it says sodomy is sin. Do you see a difference? Why?

Notes

4. Sin is sin and it is not your identity – sexual or otherwise. Just because you have identified with a sin in the past, does not mean you must continue to do so. For example, alcoholics, kleptomaniacs, food addicts, and compulsive gamblers recognize that they have temptations that have become unmanageable, but they also recognize that acting on those temptations are unhealthy and not in God's plan for their life. Can you see your sexual sin as separate from your identity?

5. Are you willing to lay your sexuality at God's feet and let God guide your decisions on this topic?

Exercise:

Look up and write down these scriptures that will encourage your beloved identity in Christ!

1. I am a saint (Ephesians 1:1; 1 Corinthians 1:2; Philippians 1:1; Colossians 1:2)
2. I am the salt of the earth (Matthew 5:13)
3. I am the light of the world (Matthew 5:14)
4. I am a branch of the true vine, able to bear much fruit in Christ (John 15:1,5)
5. I have been appointed by Christ to bear lasting fruit (John 15:16)
6. I was chosen before the creation of the world to be seen as holy and blameless (Ephesians 1:4)
7. I am Christ's ambassador (2 Corinthians 5:20)
8. I have the right to come boldly near the throne of God to receive mercy and grace when I need it (Hebrews 4:16)

How Satan Exploits Our Weaknesses

Your brokenness and the people around you are the reason for your pain. There is no "Satan" trying to harm and destroy you.	Vs.	There is an enemy of our souls, Satan, seeking to leverage our hurts and the lies we believe in order to draw us away from God.

Examples of What the Enemy Wants You to Think:

- I am my own problem.
- I'm worthless.
- I'm hopeless because I am just a defective person.
- My mess can't ever be fixed.
- There is no "God" to redeem me.
- There is no way to improve my future.
- I am only as worthy as my worst experience.
- I am only as worthy as my last experience.
- How people treat me determines my value.
- There is nothing beyond what I see and feel every day.
- How I feel about myself is the truth.

God's Truth Says:

"It would be better for him if a millstone were hung around his neck, and he were thrown into the sea, than that he should offend one of these little ones." – Luke 17:2 (NKJV)

Everyone can find security in Christ to prevent these three types of exploitation:

Physical
- "And masters, treat your slaves in the same way. Do not threaten them, since you know that he who is both their Master and yours is in heaven, and there is no favoritism with him." – Ephesians 6:9
- "'You shall not cheat your neighbor, nor rob him. The wages of him who is hired shall not remain with you all night until morning." – Leviticus 19:13
- We were designed to be the temple of the Holy Spirit. We have intrinsic value because we were created in God's image. We deserve to be treated with respect.
- When we're struggling physically, all the other problems tend to feel dramatically worse. Satan will kick us while we're down. He wants to take advantage in every area he can.

Notes

Emotional

- "Be anxious for nothing, but in everything, by prayer and petition, with thanksgiving, present your requests to God. And the peace of God, which surpasses all understanding, will guard your hearts and your minds in Christ Jesus." – Philippians 4:6-7 (BSB)
- We need to claim the resources we have available in Christ to guard us and fight back when Satan is attacking. Run to God with your negative emotions. Reach out to safe counselors, pastors, sponsors, or life coaches.
- There is hope for improvement. Improvement may take a range of support or intervention depending on the severity of the damage we're dealing with.
- Emotions affect us, but they do not define us. We need to feel, be aware, recognize, process and choose the direction we go regardless of our emotions.

Spiritual

- God's heart is LOVE, healing, redemption, hope, and joy. If the spiritual interaction is pushing you away from God rather than lovingly drawing you toward Him, there may be a problem.
- Cults and spiritual abusers will use scripture to put you down, control you, and separate you from the love and grace found in a relationship with God through Christ. Cults suck you in so they can control and use you. This can be very damaging.
- Beware of scripture being used out of context, or used without the heart and theme of God behind it. Jesus came to set you free, not so you could be silenced, controlled, or shamed.
- One of the more frequently misused scriptures is the text: "wives submit to your husbands." (Ephesians 5:22) Remember, God asks married couples first to "submit yourselves one to another." (Ephesians 5:21)
- Respect your elders or authority figures, but not at the cost of who you are as a child of God. You obey and follow God first. Always.
- "But when I saw that they were not straightforward about the truth of the gospel, I said to Peter before them all, "If you, being a Jew, live in the manner of Gentiles and not as the Jews, why do you compel Gentiles to live as Jews?" – Galatians 2:14 (NKJV)
- Many times, man will take God's guidelines and add to them in ways that are heavy and controlling. Like the Jews making the Sabbath an overloading requirement, but Jesus said that the Sabbath was made for man, not man for the Sabbath.
- The fruits of the Spirit in scripture will give you the balance to the commandments.

Listen to This Song:

"Priceless" by For King And Country

Notes

Questions to Help You Process This Concept:

1. Have you ever been physically exploited? At work? At home? At church? Where you've had no feeling of control over what you HAD to do? The work you had to perform?

2. Have you ever been emotionally exploited? Has a narcissist ever emotionally or mentally manipulated or controlled you? Has anyone kept you on an emotional roller coaster?

3. Have you ever been sexually exploited? By a boyfriend? Spouse? A friend, neighbor, family member, or stranger? Were you ever touched inappropriately? Groped or grabbed without your consent? Coerced to have sexual contact when you weren't actually wanting it?

4. Have you ever been spiritually exploited? Told that you had to do stuff to qualify for God's love or redemption? Told that if you didn't serve someone or the church a certain way that you were not going to heaven or that God would be upset with you? Was performance a requirement for eternal salvation?

Notes

5. Have you ever felt that others took advantage of you when you were weak or sick? When you froze and couldn't say "No?" Have you felt like you couldn't set boundaries because they were never respected?

Exercises:

1. Write down the people who you can't say "no" to.

2. Write down the situations where you feel like you're always obligated to do what's requested regardless of how you feel.

3. Write down the ways you've been told that you have to earn your salvation or submit to a person to be loved by God—including behavior, dress, activities, etc.

4. If you've answered any of these questions with a person, situation or way, we recommend that you borrow or buy the book *Boundaries* by Dr. Henry Cloud and Dr. John Townsend. This book will help you see your choices and freedom more clearly and explain how you can set boundaries that will be respected.

Religion Isn't A Fix

If I could just have _____, then I'd finally get some peace.	Vs.	True peace can be found in a redemptive and loving relationship with God.

Examples of What the Enemy Wants You to Think:

- True peace is a fairy tale. I will always carry this fear and hurt.
- If I just do enough good works, then maybe God will take away the pain.
- God won't care about me until I've proven myself as worthy.
- I'm not good enough to have God intervene in my life.
- Finding peace is up to me; I have to make all the right decisions to make it all fall in line.
- If I did all the right things, then God would make my circumstances work out.
- I can't let anyone find out how much fear I have, or they'll know I'm not lovable.
- Escaping my problems is the only type of peace I'll ever have so my addiction is necessary for survival.

God's Truth Says:

"And you will seek Me and find Me, when you search for Me with all your heart." – Jeremiah 29:13 (NKJV)

Ask God to make Himself real to you.
- "'Call to Me, and I will answer you, and show you great and mighty things, which you do not know.'" – Jeremiah 33:3 (NKJV)
- God cares deeply for all His children no matter what they've done or what has been done to them. He wants to be a part of their lives.
- God is waiting for the moment you ask Him into your problems. You are not a burden or an inconvenience to Him. He's eagerly watching.
- God knows what is important to you. If you ask Him to make Himself real to you, He will do so in a very personal way. Be on the lookout for His reply. Do not be afraid to ask for confirmation if you are unsure He was personally reaching out to you.

Be honest with God about your deepest hurts and brokenness.
- "He who has My commandments and keeps them, it is he who loves Me. And he who loves Me will be loved by My Father, and I will love him and manifest Myself to him." – John 14:21 (NKJV)

Notes

- "Search me, O God, and know my heart; Try me, and know my anxieties;" – Psalm 139:23 (NKJV)
- God is familiar with every moment of your past. He's not ignorant. He's omniscient. He was there.
- Sharing with Him through a confessing prayer is what helps you to invite Him into those hurting places of your heart.
- When you create a relationship with a new friend, or seek to create a deeper relationship with an old friend, you look for ways to communicate and hang out. You share honestly about your hopes and dreams, hurts and memories. A relationship with God is built in the same way.

Spend quality time with God.
- "Draw near to God, and he will draw near to you." – James 4:8a (NKJV)
- There is a reason quality time is described as a "love language." Our time is important to us. When we share our time with a friend or family member, we are giving them a valuable commodity as we receive a valuable commodity from them.
- Open your heart in this quality time to receive what God is giving to you: love and acceptance. Over time, you'll recognize His character is consistent and His motives are pure. He just wants to help you.
- It's true that God hates sin, but He still loves the sinner. If you surrender your will to Him, He will make a way to redeem the hurt and pain of the past and heal the wounds in your heart.

Listen To This Song:

"My Life" by David Manning

Questions to Help You Process This Concept:

1. What is your fix? Is it a "good" addiction or a bad addiction? Sometimes we think that socially acceptable addictions are okay. For example: work addiction (workaholic), cleaning addiction, exercise addiction, reading addiction, etc.

Notes

2. What type of relationship do you have with God? Is it authentic or just religious?

3. Have you ever asked God to make Himself real to you? Did He show up?

4. Have you ever been completely honest with God about how you feel? Have you been too afraid to share your deepest hurts with Him? (Remember that He was there throughout your life. He knows your deepest struggles. Jesus died on the cross for us while we were still sinners. He loves us regardless.)

Exercises:

1. Write "God" on a large piece of paper.

2. Put a chair across from where you like to sit comfortably.

3. Put your "God" sign on the chair.

4. Set a timer on your phone or other timer for fifteen minutes.

Notes

5. For the fifteen minutes, sit in your chair and talk to the "God" sign like He's a person.

6. Make a commitment to talk to Him like this for fifteen minutes a day for the next week.

God Redeems What Satan Destroys

Pain and suffering always come from God as punishment. Satan isn't the culprit.	Vs.	Every good thing comes from God. Satan is the one who steals, kills, and destroys.

Examples of What the Enemy Wants You to Think:

- God is using my circumstances to punish me.
- I am not worthy of blessings.
- My life is so hard because God doesn't care about me.
- God doesn't love me because I'm in so much pain.
- Nothing seems to work out, so God must have forgotten me.
- I've sinned in my past, so God will never love or accept me.
- I'm not worthy of forgiveness.

God's Truth Says:

"The thief does not come except to **steal, kill** and **destroy**. I have come that they may have life, and that they may have it more abundantly." - John 10:10 (NKJV)

"We wrestle not against flesh and blood, but against principalities, against powers, against the rulers of darkness of this world, against spiritual wickedness in high places." - Ephesians 6:12 (KJV)

You can discern Satan's handiwork by looking for these kinds of fruit:

Loss (steal)
- The enemy can cause physical theft from a break-in. But he also incites intangible thefts like lost opportunities.
- Mentally, we fight a battle with Satan every day. He strives and tempts us to believe any lie that he can. The more lies we believe, the further he can tear us away from God's love and peace.
- Luckily, our God is bigger and literally created and owns ALL the resources that ever were. He is capable of providing everything we need, despite Satan's attempts.

Death (kill)
- Doctors generally agree that about 80% of illnesses are caused by stress, which is rooted in fear. God says He has "not given us a spirit of fear, but of power, love and

Notes

sound mind." (2 Timothy 1:7) Illness can effectively kill our dreams, hope, energy, relationships and career, as well as our bodies. And while God redeems those losses, Satan is the one who attempted to cause the death to begin with.

- Murder is too often a reality in our world. Whether on the battlefield or in the home, you can bet Satan was the instigator spreading his lies of hate.
- While it may be too late for God to redeem murder in the lives of the victims, He absolutely works to redeem the murder through the lives of those who were touched by the victim, perpetrator, or tragedy in some way.

Destruction (destroy)

- One of the most valuable ways Satan tries to destroy is through division in relationships. In other words, his strategy is to, "divide and conquer." He attempts to do this in churches, personal relationships, and with our relationship with God as well.
- Blaming and hating God or others for the brokenness inspired by Satan, only continues to help Satan's cause. It keeps us divided and closes the door to the healing and restorative work God wants to do.

Listen to This Song:

"Broken Vessels (Amazing Grace)" by Hillsong

Questions to Help You Process This Concept:

1. Have you been blaming God for the evil in the world? Or have you been recognizing that Satan is trying to steal, kill, and destroy?

2. What has Satan stolen from you that you previously attributed to God's will?

Notes

3. How have you seen God redeem a loss, murder, or destruction in someone else's life?

4. Which of the lies listed above have you believed in the past, or struggle with today?

5. Do you see how God can restore you? Your health, relationships, finances, or jobs.

Exercises:

1. Get two sheets of paper.

2. Write down good things that have happened on one and bad things on the other.

3. Thank God for everything on the good list.

4. Look at the bad list and ask God to show you the ways He has redeemed those things (personal growth, closer relationship with God, restored relationships with others, Godly character—humility, peace, etc.)

When Abuse Leads to Porn Addiction
(Casting the First Stone)

We need to judge others because they need us to tell them what they are doing wrong.	Vs.	God instructs us to love and forgive despite others' sins because we are all broken and need redemption.

Examples of What the Enemy Wants You to Think:

- I'm better than those people.
- I'm more broken than anyone else.
- What I have done is unforgivable.
- What they have done is unforgivable.
- Those sinners are just weak.
- I would never do anything so horrible.
- They are so terrible, they deserve whatever's coming to them.

God's Truth Says:

Parable of the two praying men:
"I tell you that this man (the one asking for mercy), rather than the other (thanking God he's better than others), went home justified before God. For all those who exalt themselves will be humbled, and those who humble themselves will be exalted." - Luke 18:14 (NIV)

We have all been hurt and damaged.
- "For all have sinned and fall short of the glory of God." – Romans 3:23 (NIV)
- The areas of pain, level of hurt and types of damage we've each experienced will vary from person to person.
- While we may not directly understand the exact pain and experiences of others, we can empathize with them because we've each known pain in this broken world.
- We can all relate to choosing a coping mechanism when we hurt. But hurt and trauma at a young age leaves us especially inclined to choosing poor coping mechanisms later in life.

We are all longing for love and acceptance.
- Love and acceptance are universally acknowledged as basic human needs. God built us to be in community and loved and accepted by Him.
- When we don't know how to get these needs met, we become increasingly desperate. That desperation can lead to destructive decisions we would not have chosen.

Notes

- An addiction starts as a way to ease the pain, but can escalate into a dependence before we know what has happened.
- "But whoever keeps His word, in him the love of God has truly been perfected. By this we know that we are in Him." - 1 John 2:5 (NASB)

We have all been self-righteous and judgmental.
- "You hypocrite, first take the log out of your own eye and then you will see clearly to take the speck out of your brother's eye." – Matthew 7:5 (ESV)
- None of us is perfect. We have all sinned. We have all committed the sin of judging others.
- By taking our thoughts captive, we can more readily recognize when judgment wants to creep in. Then we can use empathy and scripture to change our perspective.
- Judgment may seem like a sin that is "better" than others, but keep in mind, Jesus only spoke harshly with the self-righteous while on earth. The lost and hurting sinners he forgave, healed, instructed and encouraged.

Listen to This Song:

"Jesus, Friend of Sinners" by Casting Crowns

Questions to Help You Process This Concept:

1. Have you ever judged those around you? In what areas?

2. Have you ever felt superior to others because your sin didn't look like theirs? List some specifics.

Notes

3. Have you felt like your sins were worse than others and not worthy of forgiveness? In what areas?

4. Have you made bad choices looking for love and acceptance in the wrong places? Describe.

5. Have you ever truly reached out to God in desperation and felt Him meet you in your brokenness? When?

Exercises:

1. List two examples of where you've fallen short and needed compassion and forgiveness in the past.

2. List two places where you have been harsh in your judgment of someone else.

3. Bring both these lists to God. Ask God to:
   a. Forgive your broken areas.
   b. Give you compassion for other people's broken areas.

Was It My Fault?

It was my fault that someone hurt me. There must be something wrong with me.	Vs.	It is always the perpetrator's fault. A victim can't make a perpetrator hurt them. It's NOT the victim's fault.

Examples of What the Enemy Wants You to Think:

- It was my fault.
- I should have known better.
- If I had just been better, I wouldn't have been hurt.
- It was my fault because I didn't stop it from happening.
- It was my fault because I didn't fight it hard enough.
- I was the one who made them angry, so it's my fault.
- My body responded, so I must have wanted it to happen.
- I must have done something wrong, dressed wrong, or acted wrong for this abuse to have happened to me.
- The abuser said I made them do this to me, so it must me my fault.

God's Truth Says:

"He (the Devil) was a murderer from the beginning, not holding to the truth, for there is no truth in him. When he lies, he speaks his native language for he is a liar and the father of lies." - John 8:44 (NIV)

"The thief comes only to steal, kill and destroy." - John 10:10 (NIV)

Every victim can stop blaming themselves by identifying these lies:

I set myself up for it.
- Even if you make decisions that put you in a potentially vulnerable position, the responsibility rests solely upon the person who violated you.
- How you dressed is never a valid reason for a perpetrator to hurt you. Neither is your level of sobriety or intoxication. Neither is your past sexual history.
- Victims are not responsible even if the perpetrator blames them.
- Children are never at fault in abuse situations. It is the older person or adult's responsibility to not hurt nor harm the child regardless of the child's actions or words.
- Loving discipline is not abusive, it is instructive and redemptive with consequences that are appropriate and wrapped in love and kindness.

Notes

I didn't say no.
- Coercion and threats make it impossible to say no in many circumstances.
- Our bodies are not just wired for "fight or flight" responses to threats. Fawning is another natural instinct that arises. When we fawn, we will actually go along with anyone we feel threatened by. This is not a choice, it is a reflex we cannot stop in the moment.
- If you were not willingly and gladly participating, you were a victim. If the person threated to leave you, not love you, hurt you or someone else, hurt themselves, or any other threats—you were a victim.

I enjoyed it.
- If your body has a pleasurable sexual response, even when you did not want to be in the situation, the response was not a sin and it did not mean that you wanted the experience.
- Physical pleasure alone is not love.
- A pleasurable physical response during unwanted abuse is not healthy joy nor connection, nor love. It is a chemical response, a reflex, that has been hard wired into your body.

Listen to This Song:

"Everlasting Love" by CeCe Winans

Questions to Help You Process This Concept:

1. Has anyone ever hurt you and then blamed you for it? Who and when?

2. Have you ever blamed yourself for someone else abusing you?

Notes

3. What lies have you believed about yourself as a victim of abuse? Did you take the perpetrator's blame onto yourself?

4. Have you ever felt you were at fault because you froze and didn't know how to say no?

5. Did you somehow have positive physical or emotional feelings or get something out of an abusive situation? (pleasure, money, benefits) Did this make you feel more guilt or shame? (It's still never your fault. No matter what. Especially if you are a child or triggered into a child trauma freeze.)

Exercises:

1. Write "my fault" in the center of a sheet of paper.

2. Brainstorm anything that you believe to be your fault and write it on the sheet.

3. Ask God to show you any place that was actually your fault. Circle them.

4. Repent and ask God for forgiveness for each circled item.

Notes

5. Accept your complete forgiveness for each area you repented for.

6. Now, scribble out everything on the page including the circled and un-circled items.

7. Then destroy the page.

8. Thank God for His forgiveness and freedom from fault, guilt, and shame for every item written and destroyed.

It's Never Too Late to Find God

You've messed up too much for God to accept you any longer no matter how sincere you are in running to Him.	Vs.	God will accept you with open arms when you turn to Him and repent - no matter what your past looks like.

Examples of What the Enemy Wants You to Think:

- I've sinned way too many times to be welcome into God's family.
- I'm too messed up to be loved by God.
- I'm a lost cause.
- I should just give up because there's no way I'm getting into heaven.
- I'm worthless to God.
- How could God love me with my past?
- I'm damaged beyond repair.
- I'm unlovable.

God's Truth Says:

Everyone can come home to God for these three reasons:

God loves you unconditionally; no matter who you are.
- God created all of us in His image. He loves us because He is love; not because of who we are or what we've done.
- Jesus died for all of our sins.
- Despite whether we feel loved or not, God is constant in His love for us.
- If others told you that God doesn't love you for any reason, this is false. Either they were intentionally trying to do harm or they were deceived by the enemy's lies.
- "While we were yet sinners, Christ died for us." Romans 5:8 (KJV)

He's always within reach; no matter where you've gone.
- God is everywhere, so there is no way to get away from Him and His love.
- Even when we have turned our backs on God repeatedly, His love is available in an instant.
- If you went in the opposite direction that God asked you to go, His love continues in your rebellion, even when His blessings may not follow your path.
- "Nor height nor depth, nor any other creature shall be able to separate us from the love of God which is in Christ Jesus our Lord." - Romans 8:39 (KJV)

Notes

He doesn't condemn you; no matter what you've done.
- "Neither do I condemn thee: go, and sin no more." John 8:11b (KJV)
- The Holy Spirit gently convicts us and encourages us to follow God's plan and commandments at every point in our journey. He does not shame or punish us to teach us a lesson or set things right.
- We are forgiven, not because we've done anything to deserve it, but because Jesus paid the ultimate price for our sins. He's just waiting for us to accept His total forgiveness so we can walk in freedom.
- There are no exceptions to God's offer of forgiveness. He sacrificed His son once for ALL His children.

Listen to This Song:

"Home" by Chris Tomlin

Questions to Help You Process This Concept:

1. Have you ever felt like you've done something that was unforgivable?

2. Have you stayed away from God in an area because you felt you weren't worthy to go home to Him?

3. Have you accepted God's forgiveness, but refused to forgive yourself? (Truly accepting God's forgiveness means total forgiveness. Jesus' blood covers ALL your sins.)

Notes

4. Have you felt Christians judge or condemn you for your past or present? (Jesus said He didn't condemn. Conviction restores you to God. It doesn't separate you from Him.)

5. What is stopping you from running to God with all your heart? (Don't let anything get in your way of His love and healing.)

Exercises:

1. Write a list of what you feel is coming between you and your loving Father God.

2. Repent for anything on that list that was your responsibility.

3. Accept your forgiveness from God for EVERYTHING on the list.

4. Destroy the list. Permanently. (Burn, flush, shred.)

5. Find something beautiful to put on that will symbolize your value in accepting the forgiveness given to you by God through the blood of Jesus (crown, jewelry, pretty outfit, flowers, etc.).

Burned Baby Becomes Ex-Victim

Once a victim, you'll always be a victim. There's no true healing available, just better coping skills.	Vs.	Any victim can become an Ex-Victim through God's miraculous healing because Christ died on the cross.

Examples of What the Enemy Wants You to Think:

- This will never stop hurting.
- PTSD is going to ruin my life forever.
- I'm triggered into dysfunction no matter what I do.
- This hurts too much to ever improve.
- They ruined my life when they abused me.
- No one could love me now.
- I must be defective.
- My past is so messed up that there's no hope for my future.
- I might as well enjoy my addictions, because that's all I'll ever have.

God's Truth Says:

"So you are no longer a slave, but God's child; and since you are His child, God has made you also an heir." Galatians 4:7 (NIV)

Every victim can become an ex-victim by employing these three strategies:

Forgiveness
- Without forgiveness, it is virtually impossible to heal emotional wounds.
- Emotional wounds keep us emotionally handicapped, just as physical wounds keep us physically handicapped.
- Without healing, we're vulnerable to easily becoming a victim again. Don't continue to let un-forgiveness, hatred, and bitterness make you a victim forever. Forgive for your own sake and take a step closer toward shutting the door to future abuse.
- Forgiveness shuts the door to self-abuse because accepting Christ's forgiveness for ourselves takes away the need to punish ourselves. We are free to love.
- The Lord's Prayer: "And forgive us our debts, as we forgive our debtors." - Matthew 6:12 (KJV)

Worship
- Worship helps you get filled with God's strength and love as your source. Your focus moves off of you and your problems, and onto God and His love.

Notes

- Worship also helps you to stand strong on the solid ground of God's promises. Satan's lies will tell you you're hopeless. Worship helps you see God's value and your value as His child.
- "For this reason I kneel before the Father...I pray that out of his glorious riches he may strengthen you with power through his Spirit in your inner being, so that Christ may dwell in your hearts through faith." – Ephesians 3:14-17 (NIV)

Giving Back
- Serving God and His children out of love – makes us active contributors. When we're focused on others, we're not wallowing in self-pity.
- We can find our purpose, despite the harm done to us. Leaving the brokenness behind gives us the ability to grow and continue healing.
- "And the King will say, 'I tell you the truth, when you did it to one of the least of these my brothers and sisters, you were doing it to me!'" - Matthew 25:40 (NLT)

Listen to This Song:

"Stronger" by Mandisa

Questions to Help You Process This Concept:

1. Do you feel like you're in a repeating cycle of abuse? How?

2. Have you internalized the abuse and started hurting yourself? How?

3. Have you ever tried worship as a way to break through the darkness of abuse and victimization? What worship music do you like best?

Notes

4. Have you ever stepped out of your pain by helping others? Where and how?

5. Have you ever been able to see yourself as an Ex-Victim? When and where?

Exercises:

1. Spend thirty minutes listening to worship music and reflecting on God's ability and willingness to heal your emotional and physical wounds.

2. Make a list of the people you still need to forgive.

3. Make a list of the things you need to forgive yourself for.

4. For the next week, every day, claim forgiveness for each item on both lists individually.

5. Intentionally do something kind for a friend or neighbor sometime this week.

Playboy Bunny Becomes Women's Advocate

The people around you and their opinions determine your value.	Vs.	God determines your value and can show you how He sees you.

Examples of What the Enemy Wants You to Think:

- I must not be beautiful because I've never been told I was beautiful.
- My family has to say I'm beautiful, because they are my family. That doesn't mean it's true.
- If others see that I am too tall/fat/skinny/short, etc. then it must be true.
- There is something wrong with my body.
- God made a mistake when He made me.
- Compared to others, I just don't measure up.
- I'll never look like a model, so I'm not good enough.
- If only _____ was different on my body, I'd be accepted and loved.
- I was just born ugly.
- Without physical beauty, I am nothing.
- If I'm not pretty/handsome enough, I'm worthless.

God's Truth Says:

Everyone can choose to see their value through God's eyes by focusing on these three viewpoints:

Others' viewpoint
- Others see us through their own brokenness first. Sometimes they see us as being more than we really are because they've put us on a pedestal. Other times they don't see our value because they're hung up on their own list of value requirements that are based on superficial standards.
- Their opinion is not definitive truth. How others see us has nothing to do with our intrinsic value as children of the Creator. What we look like, how smart we are, what we can do—these have nothing to do with our value in God's eyes.
- People can be hateful with their bullying or hurtful comments. Many times, their words and behaviors are based in their own pain or insecurity and have nothing to do with you, especially if it appears their intention is to hurt you.
- "Death and life are in the power of the tongue." – Proverbs 18:21 (KJV)
- Being preoccupied with how others see you is a distraction from your relationship

Notes

with God that brings unrest and fear. Release their opinions to God. Trust He is big enough to protect you and work out His plans despite what others believe about you. Once you trust Him with their viewpoints, you will be free to focus on God and how He sees you.

Our viewpoint

- We see ourselves through our own brokenness and other's brokenness. Our viewpoints have been obscured by decades of damage that's built up in layers. Like dark sunglasses, it can make it very difficult to have any clarity at all.
- On our own, we are never enough. We always see flaws. Because we were born in "trespasses and sins," we are not capable of seeing the beautiful original design our Creator lovingly created us with. Because of Christ's blood, we have been washed clean. Now, we just need to see it.
- If we've agreed with the world, we will not see clearly. The world around us blasts messages designed to show us we're not enough so that we will be consumers of all the solutions being sold to improve us. The marketing works, right? We are seeing ourselves through the marketing strategies of professionals instead of through the intrinsic value system God planned.
- "Out of the abundance of the heart his mouth speaks." – Luke 6:35 (NKJV)
- Keeping your heart open to God and His viewpoint will help you see and speak from a heart that sees and appreciates your value and the value of others.

God's viewpoint

- He sees us as His unique creation without comparison to others.
- God has made each one of His children uniquely according to His plan. Cultures have different collective opinions about beauty, but God's determination is timeless without broken influences and opinions.
- He sees us clothed in Jesus' righteousness.
- "Lord, to whom shall we go? You have the words of eternal life." – John 6:68 (NIV)

Listen to This Song:

"Hey Girl" by Nicole C. Mullen.

Questions to Help You Process This Concept:

1. What are the messages you've received from friends, family, or bullies about your value? Did they align with God's valuation of you?

Notes

2. Have you ever accepted what others have said about your body or value, even if it was a lie?

3. How have you reinforced the damaging viewpoints of others with your thoughts, words, actions, or self-criticism?

4. How has comparing yourself to others prevented you from seeing yourself clearly?

5. In what area have you insisted that God got it wrong when He made you? Have you ever considered that this is telling God that you know better than Him? (Read Job 38:4-11)

Notes

Exercises:

1. Watch a short video of Nick Vujicic, who has no arms nor legs, which you can find on Youtube.

2. Go stand in front of a mirror (Don't freak out. You will survive this.).

3. Put your hands on your head and thank God for giving you your head. (If this exercise makes you cry, then it's especially important that you complete it.)

4. Touch your face and thank God for designing your face.

5. Touch your lips and thank God for designing your lips.

6. Continue touching each area of your anatomy—thanking God for His design. Even the "flaws" or "mistakes" need to be included (God doesn't make mistakes. If we let Him, God will use every part of us for His glory.).

7. As we accept and thank God for creating us, part by part, we open the door to seeing ourselves through His eyes.

Choosing Your God-Given Passion

You become whatever happens to you.	Vs.	God created you with talents and a purpose designed to glorify Him, which you can choose to follow.

Examples of What the Enemy Wants You to Think:

- I have no purpose in life.
- I've missed out on my purpose and there's no getting it back.
- It's too late to follow God's calling.
- I'm only here for one purpose.
- I have to do or become what others expect from me.
- I don't have a purpose or calling.
- God won't let me do what I want.

God's Truth Says:

God wants us to operate in faith and trust.
- The world is scared of the unknown, but we can trust an unknown future to a known God.
- The world will discourage anything outside the norm, but God calls us to be set apart for His purposes.
- "As for you, you were dead in your transgressions and sins, ... when you followed the ways of this world and of the ruler of the kingdom of the air, the spirit who is now at work in those who are disobedient." – Ephesians 2:1-2 (NIV)

God operates out of freedom rather than bondage.
- God wants to change the brokenness in our lives through His healing.
- God wants us to be free of the enemy and his lies, so we can thrive and flourish.
- God wants us to break chains, not stay locked up in them. When we're free of the bondage, we can look to Him to use us for the purpose He created us to fulfill.
- "He has delivered us from the domain of darkness and transferred us to the kingdom of his beloved Son." – Colossians 1:13 (ESV)

God has a specific plan for you to fulfill on this earth.
- He designed you for that specific plan. No one else was created to complete your God-given purpose. You are uniquely designed for His purposes.
- We are given opportunities to help others come to Christ and heal, but we will miss out on that if we simply follow the world's ideas for our lives.

Notes

- We are in sin if we do NOT follow God's calling (even out of fear). Fear directs us to follow the enemy's plan for our lives. Everything that isn't obedience to God is sin. (Romans 6:16)
- Choose to find and follow God's specific plan for your life so you can glorify God here on earth.
- "I have given them your word and the world has hated them, for they are not of the world any more than I am of the world. My prayer is not that you take them out of the world but that you protect them from the evil one." – John 17:14-15 (NIV)

Listen to This Song:

"God Help Me" by Plumb

Questions to Help You Process This Concept:

1. Are you walking in your God-given calling? What is it?

2. Has God given you a dream that you haven't fulfilled yet? What is it?

3. Has something been stopping you from walking in your calling? What?

4. If you don't know what your calling is, have you asked God? What is He telling you?

Notes

5. Have you shared your vision or calling with others and had them not support you? Did that derail you?

Exercises:

God never has just one purpose in mind for your life. You can serve Him in different capacities in different seasons. If you are not sure where He is guiding you in this season, complete the following exercise:

1. On a blank piece of paper, brainstorm all of the things that you'd like to do with your life.

2. Consider each one individually.

3. God's purpose for our lives is always to grow in love toward Him and others. Separate out the goals that are entirely for personal gain, comfort, power, fame, or money as they do not honor God's heart.

4. Pray over the remaining ideas. Put each one at the foot of the cross and give Him permission to guide your purpose, rather than asking God to bless your personal plan and expectations.

5. Spend the next week (or longer) in prayer, listening to how God leads you.
   a. He may use people, places, or things around you to give confirmation and bring direction.
   b. If the timing is not right, God may not give you a clear answer on any specific idea you have written down. That's okay. Keep praying, and He will guide you when the time comes. Moses was eighty before his story really got rolling. As long as you are breathing, God still has a purpose for you.

6. While you are waiting for answers on a larger calling, God has a purpose for you today as well. Consider where you are in this season.
   a. Brainstorm how you can love God and love others in your regular, daily life.
   b. Commit to adding these small actions to your regular routine.

Coping With Unexpected Death

If you lose someone you love, your life is over.	Vs.	God can carry you through any hardship or pain because His love is greater than any devastation.

Examples of What the Enemy Wants You to Think:

- Without them, there is no point to living.
- I can't handle this pain, so I'm going to end it all.
- No one can live through this pain.
- My life is over.
- How can I ever be happy again?
- I'm never going to enjoy life again.
- I will always be lonely from here on out.
- Who else could ever love me?

God's Truth Says:

Keep an eternal perspective.
- There is pain and trouble on this earth because of sin. Loss and death are a part of that pain. We all wish we could run away from the pain or that God would keep it from ever happening.
- Instead, God meets us in the pain. He carries us through the heartache. He hurts with us. John 11:35 "Jesus wept." After Lazarus died. They were friends. Jesus felt the pain of loss even though He knew where Lazarus was.
- We get to run to him with our pain and loss and let Him draw us closer to Him in those devastating, raw times.
- "I have set the Lord always before me; because he is at my right hand, I shall not be shaken." - Psalm 16:8 (ESV)

Surrender your pain to God.
- "He heals the brokenhearted and binds up their wounds." - Psalm 147:3 (NKJV)
- God is the only one who can truly heal these hurts. Other options and coping mechanisms can distract or even do harm.
- Run to God in the pain. Trust Him to carry you through it. Ask Him to heal your heartache. He will. In His time.

Notes

Choose gratitude.
- "Do not be anxious about anything but in every situation, by prayer and petition, with thanksgiving, present your requests to God. And the peace of God which transcends all understanding, will guard your hearts and your minds in Christ Jesus." - Philippians 4:6-7 (NIV)
- Self-pity wants us to only see the hurt we are experiencing. But God says to go to Him with thanksgiving. That doesn't mean we don't feel the pain. It means we are still grateful to Him for the good things and people in our lives.

Listen to This Song:

"I Will Rise" by Chris Tomlin

Questions to Help You Process This Concept:

1. Do you have loss or unexpected pain in your story? What is it?

2. Are you asking God to show you the eternal impact of the earthly pain?

3. Do you see God's heart hurting with you? Do you know that He wants to be with you through the pain?

Notes

4. Have you surrendered your pain to God? From the deepest places in your heart? Do you trust Him with the pain?

5. Have you asked God to heal the pain of loss? Are you trusting Him to walk you through the grieving and pain?

6. Have you been able to focus on the blessings God has given you? Even when you feel devastated? Not to avoid the pain, but to keep it from sinking into self-pity and despair?

Exercises:

1. After listening to the Chris Tomlin song, "I Will Rise," take a moment and ask God to come into your pain and grief. Ask Him to help you through the grief.

2. Ask God to give you an eternal perspective on this place of pain. How might God want to use this pruning in your life to come into closer relationship with Him and further His kingdom? Think of Biblical examples or stories of how others have brought good out of similar pain.

Notes

3. Thank God for:
   a. The blessings He gave you in the past.
   b. The blessings He's providing today, in the present.
   c. List any blessings you may have taken for granted in the past.
   d. Consider how you might be a blessing to others.

Performance Doesn't Bring Life

It's my responsibility to perform perfectly on my own, even if it's a façade.	Vs.	God brings life through us rather than expecting us to manufacture strength and wisdom on our own.

Examples of What the Enemy Wants You to Think:

- It's safer to pretend like I am perfect.
- People will only like me if I keep up the persona.
- I would be rejected or laughed at if I show any weakness.
- God wants our obedience, so I have to make sure I do everything right.
- If I mess up, God may not love me or at least want to punish me.
- If I only tried harder, then I might be good enough to help more people.
- It's my responsibility to have the right words to say to encourage others.
- It's all on my shoulders to make God and others accept me.
- I can't make God look bad, so I have to be perfect.

God's Truth Says:

"And the world is passing away along with its desires, but whoever does the will of God abides forever." – 1 John 2:17 (ESV)

We can only give the love we receive.
- "Whoever does not love does not know God, because God is love." - 1 John 4:8 (NIV)
- God did not design humans to be their own source of wisdom, strength, or love. He designed us to receive those gifts in abundance by continuously being in relationship with Him in worship, in prayer, and in the word.
- You may have heard the phrase, "you cannot pour out of an empty cup." Well, in this analogy God designed us to be His cups - or vessels – He did not also design us to be the water in those cups.
- He pours His living water into us. That is the same water we can pour out into others' lives.
- If we are trying to manufacture love, wisdom, or strength from our own performance, it will be human - broken. When we pour out love, wisdom, and strength, that we first received from God, we are giving gifts that are eternally blessed.

Notes

We can only step in a life-giving direction if we are listening.
- "...rather, blessed *are* they that hear the word of God, and keep it." - Luke 11:28 (KJV)
- When we assess the world around us, we are limited to our perspective and knowledge alone. We have no ability to see how others' lives and future decisions may impact us down the road. But God does. God has the ability to understand every perspective and what will happen in the future. Why would you rely on your own limited knowledge if you have access to an all-knowledgeable God that is working for your good?

We can only bear fruit if it comes from God.
- "A good tree cannot bear bad fruit, and a bad tree cannot bear good fruit." - Matthew 7:18 (NIV)
- "Abide in me, and I in you. As the branch cannot bear fruit of itself, except it abide in the vine; no more can ye, except ye abide in me." - John 15:4 (ESV)
- We are not capable of living self-sufficiently. He never asks us to have the power to do it all on our own. God asks us to be His hands and feet to bring His love story to the world.
- If we ask God to bless our plans, then we are asking Him to bless a broken plan without the full knowledge of His best for us. If we, instead, ask Him to show us His plan for our eternal best, then our obedience will produce the fruit that comes from God – good fruit.
- The more we look to God for direction and walk according to His will, we can be invited deeper and deeper into His plan. We can see first-hand how God orchestrates our words and deeds to show others that He cares and He is listening.

Listen to This Song:

"Strong Enough" by Matthew West

Questions to Help You Process This Concept:

1. Have you ever striven to produce love, wisdom, or strength in your own power, without God?

Notes

2. How did your attempts to perform ultimately harm you or others around you when you ran out of steam?

3. In what areas of your life are you still trying to produce good fruit without seeking God's will and strength to carry you through?

4. What would it look like for you to listen to God's plan in those areas and follow His prompting rather than your own?

5. Have you seen yourself as an empty vessel ready for God to fill and work through?

Exercises:

1. Get a piece of paper.

2. Make a list of all the things you've done right in your life.

Notes

3. Circle the ones that you did in your own strength.

4. Which ones have you done only through God's power? Where you know you couldn't have done it in your own strength?

5. What things did you do wrong because you weren't capable of doing them right?

6. Take both lists to God. Surrender them to Him. Repent for any areas where you thought you were doing stuff in your own strength. Thank Him for the areas where you let Him work through you.

Walking by Faith, Not by Sight

I need to know and understand everything to move forward.	Vs.	God wants us to trust His eyes instead of our own sight or understanding.

Examples of What the Enemy Wants You to Think:

- It's too hard because I can't see the outcome.
- But I don't know how this can possibly work.
- God hasn't shown me everything, so I can't obey yet.
- This doesn't make any sense to me, so I can't...
- I can't make this happen, so I'm not going to try.
- If I can't control the outcome, it's too risky to move.
- But I might lose _____.

God's Truth Says:

Recognize your eyes are limited.
- "For we walk by faith, not by sight." – 2 Corinthians 5:7 (NKJV)
- Walking by faith is using more sight than eyes.
- The Bible tells us there is a spiritual realm that exists beyond what we can see and hear.
- If we live our lives only by what we see and hear and feel, then we are ignoring a large part of our actual reality. Spiritual realities are longer lasting and have more serious consequences than the physical plain alone.
- We must consider these spiritual realities now in our everyday decision making in order to align ourselves with God and receive His protection and walk in His will.

Recognize God wants your eternal best.
- God is trustworthy because His heart has always been to restore and redeem our brokenness.
- Even before Adam and Eve were kicked out of the Garden of Eden, God had a plan to restore us and spend eternity with Him in heaven. He has the same plan for redemption and restoration in your own story; and He will lead you into that plan if you listen and trust Him.
- "And we know that in all things God works for the good of those who love him, who have been called according to his purpose." – Romans 8:28 (NIV)

Notes

Recognize you will need to obey first and understand later.
- Often, we freeze or refuse to move forward into the unknown out of fear.
- But, if God is asking us specifically to move forward we can rest assured He has a plan for the consequences.
- Even if the earthly, physical consequences are loss and/or emotional pain, we can still rest in the assurance that God's plan goes beyond the short-term of this life and stretches into the spiritual and eternal realm.

Listen to This Song:

"Walk by Faith" by Jeremy Camp

Questions to Help You Process This Concept:

1. Have you ever watched God do things you never thought were possible? When?

2. How have you seen things through the eyes of faith when it didn't match reality?

3. Have you ever felt like you had to strategize everything because God might not know how to take care of all the details? Did that stress you out?

Notes

4. Has God told you something that you've refused to obey because you couldn't figure out all the moving parts? What specifically?

5. Have you ever just obeyed God and let Him work out the details? When? How did that work out?

Exercises:

1. Get a piece of paper.

2. Write down anything you feel God has asked you to do, but you've been too scared of the consequences. This can be something as simple as speaking the truth in love or making amends or as unconventional as starting a television show.

3. Lift each one of these items up in prayer. Tell God what you would like to do, but then let Him know that ultimately, you'll surrender to what He wants of you.

4. Pick the top two or three that you feel God asking you to do immediately.

5. Listen for His encouragement or instructions. You may feel overwhelmed by the Holy Spirit on how to move next, or you may not receive a response at all. That's okay. The important part is to listen and ask for confirmation of where you are to step next.

Notes

6. Once you feel you have a peace in your spirit, write down the next step you will take and the date on which you will do it. (Note: you can still experience fear about the next step while being confident in what God is asking of you.)

7. If you need help, ask an accountability partner or mentor to help keep you accountable and talk through the experience afterward.

God Is My Only Provider

I have to find or create my own provision so that God doesn't have to be bothered.	Vs.	God has all of the resources and has the ability to provide me with any and all that He sees fit.

Examples of What the Enemy Wants You to Think:

- I am responsible for making sure me and my family are well cared for.
- God only helps those who help themselves.
- God will only provide if I perform exactly the way He wants.
- God will withhold money and resources to punish me.
- If I cannot create my own source of income, I have failed.
- If God loved me, He would give me enough money to live without stress.
- If all of my resources dry up, then it proves I am an unreliable failure.

God's Truth Says:

God is the only provider.
- Even if you thought you were providing for yourself and creating your own provision, God was still in charge of opening the doors you stepped through.
- When God places us in a season of pruning where He strips away opportunities, relationships, etc., He is ultimately drawing us back to Him. He wants us to trust in His perfect will above our own will and above the expectations of the world around us.
- In the Lord's Prayer we ask for daily bread. In addition to physical food and water, this also refers to the hope and faith we need in the midst of life's ups and down. His provision is more than the physical body. He also provides for our soul and spirit.
- "May he equip you with all you need for doing his will. May he produce in you, through the power of Jesus Christ, every good thing that is pleasing to him." - Hebrews 13:21 (NLT)

God says He will provide.
- Even when you can't see which doors will be opened (or when), God has gone before you and cleared a path.
- Our responsibility is to live according to His teachings, then listen and follow where He asks us to go. Many times, He is growing our faith or instructing us in a specific lesson by walking in a season of pruning. God's role is to provide the right connections, timing, and opportunities.

259

Notes

- "Look at the bird of the air; they do not sow or reap or store away in barns, and yet your heavenly Father feeds them. Are you not much more valuable than they?" – Matthew 6:26 (NIV)

God asks you to trust Him (even if you don't believe).
- "Therefore take no thought, saying, What shall we eat? or, What shall we drink? or, Wherewithal shall we be clothed?...But seek ye first the Kingdom of God, and His righteousness; and all these things will be added to you." - Matthew 6:31 & 33 (KJV)
- If we knew for sure our expectations of safety and provision would always be met, we wouldn't need faith, would we? Instead, God asks us to grow our relationship with Him by walking in faith.
- Perfect faith is not even required in order to trust God. In Mark 9, a man exclaims, to Jesus "Lord, I believe. Help my unbelief." This would indicate that the man was not completely faithful. You could argue that his faith was more like a mustard seed compared to his mountain of unbelief. Yet, Jesus honors the faith the size of a mustard seed because that faith is in God's power.

Listen to This Song:

"All My Hope" by Crowder (featuring Tauren Wells)

Questions to Help You Process This Concept:

1. Which one of the lies above do you resonate with the most?

2. Where has your provision come from in the past from an earthly perspective?

Notes

3. Have you ever considered that God was ultimately opening the doors to everything that has been provided for you? If not, how does this change your perspective on the past?

4. When was the last season of pruning in the area of your resources? Are you still in it? How did you respond – with faith or with fear?

5. What would it look like to step out in faith with your finances or resources even if you do not believe?

Exercises:

1. Make a list of who you think you are dependent on for your provision (include yourself).

2. Cross each one out and write God's name instead.

Fear Versus Faith

Fear is a necessary part of life that cannot be avoided.	Vs.	We can choose faith in God and His love and reject fear. His love casts out all fear and gives us a sound mind.

Examples of What the Enemy Wants You to Think:

- I need fear in order to stay motivated and be productive.
- I cannot properly love someone without worrying about them.
- It is impossible to live without fear.
- I cannot protect myself or others if I do not worry about the future.
- Fear is healthy.

God's Truth Says:

"For God has not given us a spirit of fear, but of power and of love and of a sound mind." – 2 Timothy 1:7 (NKJV)

Why we accept fear.
- We falsely believe we need fear.
- We believe the lie that worry is love.
- We falsely believe worry is helpful to achieve or motivate.

What fear does.
- Fear interrupts our body's natural ability to function properly and creates medical issues. Eighty percent of all diseases are caused by stress and fear.
- It only encourages and empowers more fear in your life.
- Fear opens the door for Satan to do more harm. If we are accepting fear as "normal" or "acceptable," then we are operating under a lie from Satan. Once we agree with Satan, we are giving him a foothold in our life.

How we change it.
- We can run to God instead of accepting fear.
- Change your focus/mind. You can choose to focus your thoughts on God's promises of joy, hope, His ultimate power, plan for our lives, and passionate love for us.

Notes

- Stand on your identity in Christ. If you make choices as if you are scared of the enemy, then you are leaving room for Satan to work. Make decisions based on the choice that you believe you are God's precious child. This will bolster your faith.
- Fear arising from a trauma or PTSD symptoms can feel overpowering and seem irrational. It may take longer to trust God and heal from these wounds, but it is not impossible. Fear does not have to win. By processing the trauma and the emotions, perhaps even with professional help, in conjunction with trusting God and His promises, eventually, the fear will leave.

Listen to This Song:

"The Break Up Song" by Francesca Battistelli

Questions to Help You Process This Concept:

1. What are the messages you've received about fear from your family of origin?

2. Some alternative words for fear include: anxious, upset, stressed, and worried. In what areas of your life have you identified with these alternative words? How does it change your perspective to realize you are holding on to fear in these areas?

3. How has fear caused you to make decisions that were not healthy/beneficial for you or others (family, coworkers, friends)? Reminder: Inaction is still a decision.

Notes

4. How has choosing fear stolen from you a "life to the full" that Jesus promised?

5. When we fully accept God's perfect love, then we fully embrace His sovereignty, His grace, ourselves, and His plan for us – even when it isn't easy or comfortable – thus casting out fear. How is fear stopping you from embracing God's perfect love for you?

6. When we have fear, then we are believing (consciously or subconsciously) God is not enough. Based on where your fears arise, where do you believe God is not enough?

Exercises:

1. Make a list of all the things and people you are afraid of.

2. Go down the list one-by-one and reflect on why each fear is unnecessary.

3. Find God's promises in His Word that reveal why these fears are unnecessary. (ex. John 16:33)

Notes

4. Bring each fear to God individually and hand it over to Him. Let Him take it from you.

5. Decide what changes you may need to make to your mindset, habits, daily life in order to walk in faith in these areas rather than fear.

What is an Ex-Victim?

Once a victim, always a victim so I'll stay a victim or just avoid admitting I've been one.	Vs.	I was a victim, but God heals and restores me regardless of the damage.

Examples of What the Enemy Wants You to Think:

- I'm permanently broken.
- No one will ever love me again.
- I deserve to be covered in shame, so I'm ashamed of myself.
- I'm worthless.
- It was my fault so I deserved it.
- I'll never feel any better.
- I'm just defective.
- I deserve to keep being a victim over and over again.
- There is no hope for me.

God's Truth Says:

"Let me not be put to shame, Lord, for I have cried out to you; but let the wicked be put to shame and be silent in the realm of the dead." - Psalm 31:17 (NIV)

God despises shame.
- Satan wants to stop you from working in God's kingdom by putting you in a corner: isolating you, removing you from relationship.
- Adam and Eve hid from God and each other in their shame rather than being in relationship with each other and God as previously.
- Hebrew 12:2 tells us Jesus "endured the cross, despising the shame."
- He had never sinned so the shame was not His, but He bore the shame of every one of us sinners!
- He despised it. Not because it hurt, but because shame comes from Satan. Jesus didn't accept the shame. We can do the same thing.
- That tells us, shame is a tool that the enemy uses. SHAME IS NOT OF THE LORD!! Shame tears you away from God.

God dispels shame.
- "I sought the Lord, and he answered me; he delivered me from all my fears. Those who look to him are radiant; their faces are never covered with shame." - Psalm 34:4-5 (NIV)

Notes

- When we turn toward God, and repent, He takes the shame off of us. We don't ever need to live in shame.
- But we have to seek Him and repent of our sins.

God replaces shame.
- "I will rescue the lame; I will gather the exiles. I will give them praise and honor in every land where they have suffered shame." – Zephaniah 3:19 (NIV)
- He wants a strong, healed relationship with you no matter what's been done to you or what you've done.
- He heals shame by replacing it with honor because of Jesus' sacrifice on the cross.

Listen to This Song:

"I Am No Victim" by Kristene Dimarco

Questions to Help You Process This Concept:

1. Have you felt shame over something that has happened to you or something you've done? If so, describe.

2. Have you struggled with admitting you were a victim? (We've all been a victim at some time in some way.)

3. Have you repented and asked God for forgiveness and then still held onto shame?

Notes

4. Have you seen the damage to your relationships that comes with carrying shame?

5. Adam and Eve were naked and not ashamed. Have you wanted the vulnerability and freedom that comes with not letting anything stand between you and God? What is still separating you from Him?

Exercises:

1. Read the poem "Ex-Victim" from Bloom In The Dark. (If you don't have a copy, download it for free at: www.bloominthedark.org/free-book)

2. Get a blank sheet of paper. (You may want to do this with a trusted mentor, pastor, or support person you trust.)

3. Ask God to bring to mind anything that may still have any shame associated with it.

4. Write down words, phrases or descriptions that represent anything you associate with feelings of shame.

5. Take the list to God. Repent for everything on it. Give Him the shame to deal with. Release the items one at a time.

6. Ask God to forgive you and remove the shame.

Notes

7. Tear the sheet up into little pieces and destroy them (in whatever way makes you feel the best without being unsafe).

8. Ask God to give you a renewed sense of innocence and freedom.

9. Thank God for all the healing and freedom He is giving you.

Additional Resources

Find healing resources,
crisis resources, and
download your free copy of

BL☼☼M
in the dark

at

Bloominthedark.org/free-book

Paula Mosher Wallace
President of Bloom In The Dark, Inc.
paula@bloominthedark.com

BL☼☼M
Forward

**A journal to renew your mind...
one day at a time.**

Use this 90 day devotional journal with
assessments and daily questions will help you
build new thought patterns, muscle memories,
and neural pathways.

RS4L.com

RS4L

RECOVERY STRATEGIES 4 LIFE

Healing for your Spirit, Soul, and Body

Unlike traditional recovery programs that only address the
soul and body, RS4L combines healing strategies for all three
parts of our being: the spirit, soul, and body.

Do you struggle with

- ☑ PTSD - Complex Trauma
- ☑ Any type of Abuse
- ☑ Addictions
- ☑ Loss
- ☑ Depression
- ☑ Fear - Stress - Anxiety
- ☑ Codependency
- ☑ Or have plateaued in their healing or recovery?

Includes

- ☑ 52 videos
- ☑ Leader's guide
- ☑ Student workbooks

About Bloom In The Dark, Inc.

Have you ever experienced a hurt so deep that it didn't qualify for a sympathy card? Did embarrassment or shame keep you from getting help or support? Do you have a loved one who's been abused?

Many women face trauma and abuse. But that doesn't have to be the end of the story. Countless women have healed from their past with God's power.

Every success story has one thing in common – hope!

We at Bloom In The Dark have seen the power of story provide the kind of hope that change lives!

Mission:

We are a 501c3 charity seeking to raise awareness about the damage caused by secret pain and abuse, and demonstrate the hope and healing found in Christ Jesus through ex-victim testimonies, connections, and tools.

Vision:

To create a culture where people choose redemption and healing in Christ Jesus so they bloom despite darkness and pain.

Values:

- LOVE: Love God, Love yourself so you can Love your neighbor
- HONESTY: Be honest with God, yourself and others especially when it hurts
- FORGIVENESS: Forgive God, yourself and others quickly
- ENCOURAGEMENT: Encourage yourself with God's Word, your words, and other's words through what you see, hear, and speak.

Learn More:

https://bloominthedark.org

Watch Bloom Today Around the World

Using the fertilizer of our past to bloom today!

Ephesians 5:8-13 (NIV)
"For you were once darkness, but now you are light in the Lord. Live as children of light (for the fruit of the light consists in all goodness, righteousness and truth) and find out what pleases the Lord. Have nothing to do with the fruitless deeds of darkness, but rather expose them. It is shameful even to mention what the disobedient do in secret. But everything exposed by the light becomes visible—and everything that is illuminated becomes a light."

Television:
(Check your local listings)

Inspiration TV - INI (*UK, Europe, Africa, Asia, The Caribbean, New Zealand, & Australia*)
Faith USA (*USA*)
NRB TV (*USA*)
Upliftv (*USA*)
CTN (*USA*)
Alpha Omega (*Romania, Moldova*)
Grace Television (*India*)
Australia Christian Channel (*Australia*)
Family 7 (*The Netherlands*)
Flow Africa (*Kwesé Channel, Africa*)
Faith Africa (*South Africa*)
Faith Terrestrial (*Eastern Cape South Africa*)
Faith UK (*UK*)
WHTN (*Middle TN*)
Sacramento Faith TV (*Sacramento, CA*)

Online Streaming:

Amazon Prime	Global 7 App
Parables	Damascus Roads
Inspiration TV App	NRB TV App
Faith Broadcasting Network App	Grace TV App

Podcast:
iTunes
iHeartRadio
YouTube
Spreaker
Sonos

Learn More:

https://bloomtodaytv.com